The Education
of
Gifted Children

David Hopkinson

THE WOBURN PRESS

First published 1978 in Great Britain by
THE WOBURN PRESS
Gainsborough House, Gainsborough Road,
London E11 1RS, England

and in the United States of America by
THE WOBURN PRESS
c/o Biblio Distribution Centre
81 Adams Drive, P.O. Box 327, Totowa, N.J. 07511

ISBN 0 7130 0156 9

W11791 £9 95. 3.80

Printed in Great Britain by The Bourne Press, Bournemouth

Contents

Preface

Modern Europe is everywhere attempting to modernise education so that it should better serve the needs of the type of society that has everywhere evolved. The underlying aim is to extend full opportunities of learning to all. The elementary education of all children and an almost totally literate population were achievements of the 19th and early 20th centuries. Now the social, political and economic demands of our time call for a compulsory education prolonged to the age of 16, and for the even more exacting vision of a society in which life-long educational opportunity is on offer. So massive an enterprise must strain the resources of all but the wealthiest nation states.

Heavily burdened by the cost of education, producers of wealth regard the educator with a critical eye. They have begun to question his competence to deliver the goods. Teachers and administrators have to submit their beliefs and practices to the tribunal of an alert public opinion. Remaining true to their ideals, they must yet be aware of lapses in performance and specific instances of neglect.

I have tried to examine what has happened to children of marked ability in a period of confusing growth and change, inspired by good intentions. I have aimed to draw attention to weaknesses of which we ought all to be aware and to which remedies must be found. It is hardly necessary to say how much I owe to friends and former colleagues with whom over the years I have discussed many of the issues raised in this book; it would be invidious to mention names. I am, however, particularly grateful to Dr. Peter Gordon for his criticism and encouragement, and to Dr. Maurice Tyerman and Dr. John Brierley for helpful information and suggestions.

CHAPTER I

Social and Personal Implications

I have in front of me a news item in a 1976 issue of *The Times* in which a mother, who is on the executive committee of a Society concerned with children with a particular disability, is reported as saying:

"[Parents] know that their children, if placed in the wrong environment, will slip very quickly downhill: that lack of stimulus . . . . . will either cause him to withdraw into obsession and self-injury or will lead to disturbed behaviour with the consequent use of drugs or isolation."

The words I have replaced with dots are, "in an over-crowded and understaffed ward"; the Society happens to be the National Society for Autistic Children. But many parents of exceptionally bright children might say something very similar.

One reason, therefore, for giving attention to the educational problems of our most able children is that much parental anxiety about them is known to exist. From this angle the very gifted are on a par with children who suffer from specific handicaps. They cause concern to parents—not invariably, but in a great many instances. It would be inhumane to ignore this concern.

The second reason is social rather than personal. Exceptional talent in its members is a matter of great importance to any community. In a modern state human ability is just as significant to the general welfare as national resources or climatic conditions. There is nothing new in this. In any crowd of human beings, at any point in history, personal dissimilarities are as certain to be seen as dissent is to be heard. And if the group is challenged from outside so that an organised collective resistance is demanded of it, the strength, cunning and executive capacity of its members will certainly be found to vary. In the interests of the group as a whole, those possessing exceptional strength, or with other skills or abilities important to the survival of all, must as a matter of common sense be looked after first, or at least receive a measure of special treatment proportionate to the size of their contribution to the collective welfare.

One of the outstanding characteristics of the modern nation state has been the elaborate specialisation and extensive division of labour on which industrial commercial and military 'development' seems so largely to depend. (States lacking these characteristics are described as underdeveloped). The growth of human knowledge and the sub-division of the process of industrial production are generally held to account for this, so that workers by hand and brain are equally affected. It would therefore appear that special aptitudes and abilities, and the harnessing of them by means of 'training' to the tasks for which they are best fitted, must be matters of importance in the modern world. At all levels in society the employment of available talent is held to be a matter to which attention has to be given. Man-power planning, i.e. attempts at manipulating human material for social ends, has become an operation acceptable to all shades of political opinion. It has been complained on the one side that the dominant party in power has neglected "reservoirs of untapped ability"; on the other that controlling the economic freedom of talented individuals has led to a "brain-drain".

Such metaphors often conceal shallow thinking or reluctance to investigate the facts. The fostering of exceptional talent and its eventual employment in the more difficult and demanding tasks on which society depends seems to be a reasonable, perhaps a mandatory, demand. That the community as a whole will suffer from failure to utilise potential assets is a proposition difficult to deny. In that case the community must share with the private persons most concerned an interest in any evidence of exceptional talent shown by children.

The concern of the individuals who care for very able children is normally heightened by their experience and their ambitions. Experience not infrequently convinces the parent or teacher that some restlessness, excitability or tension is associated with exceptional ability. A very bright child is often less easy to manage than others. Order, restraint, balance, regularity, all these are qualities which the adult tends to regard as important for the healthy development of the child. The controlled pattern of life which parents consider best for their children is often less easily established in the case of the most able. From its earliest years the most highly alert and vigorous child is likely to be more demanding than the rest. It will often appear to parents that children of this kind more readily seek out adult company. They seem to require more play materials to content them. They may be prone to sudden bursts of rage, resulting from frustration. They may more frequently be liable to trivial sickness than other children.

In short the exceptionally bright child tends to exact from parents and indeed from teachers some degree of special concern. But this special concern is notably less than that felt for handicapped or backward children at least in the early stages of education. Parents and many teachers are less able to grasp the evidence of high general ability in young children. Nor do the expert services of local authorities help very much. The point is well made by Elizabeth Hitchfield in the recommendations she introduces into her detailed study of a group of able children and their families:—

Since the 1944 Education Act stressed the responsibility of Local Education Authorities for handicapped, including maladjusted children, great progress has been made in diagnosis and educational provisions of many kinds. The agencies involved in the assessment of individual children in these categories perhaps are not yet sufficiently employed in the assessment of children who are 'exceptional' by reason of their cleverness.[1]

Clever children frequently become a focus of parental and other adult ambition. With wider prospects for the child's future in mind, greater anxieties about the parent or teacher's part in helping to secure appropriate recognition and achievement is probable. The establishment in 1966 of a National Society for Gifted Children is evidence that parents and teachers recognise that high ability in children for whom they care is something that gives rise to anxiety and may require them to seek out some special source of support.

Let us now return to the community's interest in the existence of special talent. We left off with the common-sense assertion that national assets and potential assets, human as well as material, ought to be utilised to the advantage of all; and that this principle has particular significance in complex industrial societies. But how is this interest to be expressed? What should the organs of power in a society actually do in order to realise the general aim to which all subscribe?

In the middle of the sixteenth century, England, Scotland, France and all the seventeen provinces constituting the Netherlands were governed by women as queens or regents because hereditary principles decided the allocation of such offices. In the nineteenth century government was a male preserve. Authority, power and public office had begun to pass from those who acquired them by reason of birth, or wealth, or the ability to ingratiate themselves with those thus endowed, and to be entrusted to men who possessed some kind of recognisable talent. The instruments then used for the discovery of talent now seem strange and archaic. Principally they were the reformed university degree examinations and the newly created civil service examinations. The objection to such methods was put with characteristic force by Bernard Shaw, though with the Webbs and H. G. Wells he naturally favoured the examination system in principle. The drawback to which Shaw near the end of his life drew attention was methodological: " . . . . . . the coaching of candidates for examinations becomes a profession by the aid of which any blockhead who has a good memory and has been broken-in to school drudgery can be crammed with a list of questions and ready-made answers which will enable him or her to deal with a sufficient percentage of those actually chosen for any particular examination." The system as then practised excluded in Shaw's opinion "thinkers whose memories will not retain things not worth remembering, and who cannot stomach school books, though their appetites for books which are works of art or helps to criticism of existing life are insatiable."[2]

The first half of the twentieth century brought final and total victory for the examination. Attainment replaced patronage in determining entry to almost everything worth entering from the service of the Crown to apprenticeship in most (but not all) crafts and trades. Formal examination became the rule for school leaving certificates, for admission and departure with suitable credits from university, for professional and trade qualifications. The examination system like a sewage system or the provision of street-lighting was generally accepted as a protection to the public. The attempt of a benevolent state to require that those who drove heavy vehicles on the roads, or flew passenger aircraft, or taught children, or handled radioactive materials, should know what they were doing seemed highly reasonable and beyond any possible criticism. Achieving such a purpose demanded the imposition of tests of competence. Testing and examining have become activities in which very large numbers of people are employed. The devising and administering of tests of attainment in all the subjects taught in schools is now a considerable industry.

The effect of these developments on public opinion and parental views about children's education has been profound. Not until the 1860s did the automatic association between teaching and examination take hold. As long as education was confined to a restricted section of society and was in only a small degree connected with what would now be called socio-economic status, the examination was an insignificant, or non-existent, element in the educational process. But in the build-up to the Education Act of 1870 new claims were advanced. Then one of Her Majesty's Inspectors suggested that "the studies of the classroom must be those wherein progress can be measured by examination. For examination is to the student what the target is to the rifleman; there can be no definite aim, no real training without it."[3] A hundred years later, Professor C. B. Cox wrote in the second 'Black Paper' of which he was an editor: "In a modern society education can only thrive in a context of examination . . . . . All life depends upon passing exams . . . . . To create an education system without examinations is to fail to prepare children and the students for the realities of adult life."[4]

The 20th century further strengthened the influential position alloted to testing and examining. The arrival of the educational psychologist deepened the tendency and widened the channels through which it flowed. The best known, most respected English representative of this profession was being consulted by the Consultative and Central Advisory Committees of the Board of Education throughout the 1920s and 30s. The Hadow Report on the Primary School records its debt to Cyril Burt for information about the wide variation in intelligence which children show even by the age of five and the consequent need for careful classification if their education was to be properly organised. If classifying children was so important to the arrangements to be made for teaching them, then by what method was this classification to be carried out?

In Matthew Arnold's time education was provided in accordance with a classification by social class and by the occupational prospects rising from it. And this was only challenged by the most advanced opinion of the day. But the strong tide of public opinion demanding a greater respect for social justice in education, as in other areas of human life, slowly contrived a change. Not only fairness, but also efficiency, suggested that something other than the chance of birth should determine opportunity. A claim to ability, if it could be substantiated, ought to provide at least as good a right to extended education as status in society. The problem now became one of means not of ends. For purposes of charity the deserving poor had been distinguished from the undeserving in the rigid moral climate of Victorian England without great difficulty. But for educational purposes how was this distinction to be drawn?

The principle of the competitive examination, already acceptable in other instances, became the foundation on which judgments required in a selective educational system were based. To whom then was the construction of this instrument to be entrusted? The answer lay readily to hand. Teachers in private schools, backed up since 1868 by the Report of the Taunton Commission on Endowed Schools, had acquired their modern powers over discipline, the choice of methods, the organisation and objectives of the curriculum and to heads had been assigned the appointment and dismissal of assistants. These appeared to politicians and administrators the proper principles to adopt in state-financed secondary schools. It seemed right and reasonable that teachers should take responsibility for the choice of children admitted to the secondary schools under public control; and the means of doing so must clearly be the competitive examination. The contents of syllabuses, the nature and marking of examination papers were regarded as professional matters which teachers alone were entitled to control.

This determination of power, arrived at before the First World War, and employed in the "scholarship" examination for selective secondary schools, has remained with us ever since. It is true that the Local Education Authorities have acquired a much larger share of power, largely because the organisation of entry to secondary schools became a much more complex matter after the 1944 Education Act. Educational psychologists were employed to take over responsibility for intelligence tests which constituted a one-third part of the 11+ examination, but teacher-controlled tests of attainment in English and mathematics made up the rest. When the Schools Council was set up it was as an advisory body in which teachers' power was to predominate. Proposals for reform of the curriculum and of the examination system were expected to come from its initiatives. In recent years there has in fact been much controversy, much discussion, much wasted effort and disappointment, but the basic structure of the secondary school examination remains intact. Successive Secretaries of State for Education have been unwilling to accept recommendations of the Schools Council for Curriculum and Examinations, but have not considered themselves to possess the authority that would enable them to impose changes. A national system of secondary school examination has existed for many years, but the 11+ examination, as a recent decision of the courts has shown, is a matter of local option. If an Authority, such as Tameside, wishes an examination to be conducted, nobody but the teachers can prevent it. Their failure to do so in Greater Manchester was not through lack of power but lack of unity.

This divided control could be very frustrating to politicians and also to a certain type of public servant—one who has clear ideas about the need for change in the schools and firm determination to secure the particular change for which he has a mind—but such public servants are of course extremely rare; and the interest of politicians has always been concentrated on the structure of the system rather than the contents of the syllabus.

Fairness and efficiency are the two considerations which justify and demand a system of school examinations. One affects the opportunities afforded to pupils of ability and the other the utilisation of the talents of individuals in the interests of society as a whole. As the Robbins report on higher education put it, "progress—and particularly the maintenance of our competitive position—depends . . . . . . on skills demanding special training."[5] Tests of aptitude and ability, and competitive examinations designed to select those with the capacity to profit from the best teaching over extended periods of education, provide the guarantees by means of which able children of all classes obtain their deserts. In the national interest abilities must not be wasted, as in the past they certainly were. Proven talent must be cultivated and the fruits of a national system of education employed in the national interest.

Substantial support can be found for all these propositions. Social justice for the individual and the self-protection of the community are widely held to call for methods of searching out ability, fostering its development and trying to ensure that it is suitably applied in later life. Of course there are criticisms both from the right and the left. We are told on the one hand that standards have been allowed to drop because there is a lack of vigour and purpose in the work of schools. Dangerous freedoms have been permitted to grow up. We must restore close supervision and tighter control. From the other quarter it is claimed that the widening of educational opportunity has not gone far enough, that too little is done to iron out the unequal chances to benefit from teaching which arise from differences of class and wealth. We operate a system, it is alleged, based on old assumptions about the needs of society which are no longer valid. In the words of Alvin Toffler, "Our schools face backwards towards a dying system, rather than forwards to the emerging new society."[6]

History however seems to suggest that emerging new societies have been dominated by elites and have paid a great deal of attention to structured education. In an age when human welfare increasingly depends on technology, educational drive has to be exerted in specific directions to serve national ends. A crash programme of industrialisation and scientific agriculture demands an educated group within the population. Ability to profit from education and special aptitudes in the most socially important fields of learning are as important in 'emerging' as they are in established societies. There is little need for a society, lacking modern technology, to mount systematic educational campaigns. In an illiterate society the technical knowledge required cannot extend beyond what is passed on from one generation to the next. The child, as Erikson[7] points out, becomes ready to handle the utensils, the

B

tools and the weapons of its elders in its own time; but literate people, dependent on a more elaborate technology, have to organise systematic instruction to make their children literate and numerate. Only thus can their manner of existence be secure for another generation.

In Britain the general formula for the instruction to be given at the primary stage of education has thus become language, mathematics and general knowledge. This foundation has to serve the needs of all those classified above an educationally sub-normal level. It is a programme which for the more able child may be far too limited and for the less able far too demanding. Nevertheless it has to serve as the foundation for a secondary stage designed to provide preparation for a specific area of career choice and for extended further education in the arts, sciences, or technology.

The demand for higher levels of competence and skill was among the factors that have kept far greater numbers of young people in secondary schools and was the main reason for the great expansion of further education colleges. A great deal of money had to be found for these developments and puzzling pedagogical problems had to be faced. In the main these appeared to affect the 'new' secondary school population —the average and below average children—described in the Newsom Report,[8] *Half our Future*. The major problem that obsessed educationists, in the 1960s, was the type of curriculum, the style of teaching and the most profitable school set-up for those unlikely to respond to the established secondary school tradition. Few of them could be expected to set their sights on the Ordinary Level G.C.E. examination, and so new targets, suited to their outlook and ability, had hastily to be devised. In its earlier years of existence the Schools Council, following the lead given by the Newsom Report, concentrated its resources on the production and distribution of ideas and teaching materials. A great many schools devoted much of their energies to creating acceptable and satisfying conditions for less able pupils, who had of course increased in numbers after the raising of the school-leaving age.

Often little energy was left over for the higher levels of ability. All testing and every form of examination were seen by some enthusiasts in the schools as instruments of evil employed to stamp rejection on the very children to whom the 'community' school was now opening its arms. To discriminate between levels of ability and to concentrate resources on the more able was held to promote 'divisiveness'. Early specialisation and streaming exacerbated the sense of rejection alleged to be felt by the less able. Such practices in addition were said to reflect acquisitive hierarchical middle-class values, when the real needs of society were better served by the cultivation of so-called co-operative, democratic working-class values.

It is unnecessary, however, to go all the way with those whose sentiments take these forms. There are other objections, perhaps more realistically founded, to the principle on which the 1902 Education Act was based—that the full resources necessary to provide a serious secondary stage of education should be reserved for those who manifested an ability to profit from it, taking it on its own terms. Until quite recently, it has been pointed out, Britain had won more Nobel prizes for science and literature per head of population than any other major country. This is taken by Professor Lynn, writing in Black Paper Two, to indicate that our educational system has been efficiently geared to producing an intellectual élite. Civilisation, he believes, will break down if we are diverted from this objective. But will it? Is this what has happened in America and Sweden?

In any case what are the most urgent problems of our society towards solving which all-out educational effort ought to be directed? At present it would seem that there is no more urgent issue than the economic plight of a nation with an unstable currency and relatively low productivity. The application of science is generally recognised as the principal determinant of economic success. Thus it is held that more of our able young people with the motivation and capacity to work hard, should be educated and trained as applied scientists and engineers. Why has the existing educational system, if so much to be treasured, failed us in this vital matter?

The main difficulty about all efforts to shape educational policy to the supposed interests of the community is of course the constantly changing nature of the national need and the differences of opinion that are known to exist in a democracy. Furthermore we have the almost insurmountable problem of devising and executing just and accurate procedures for identifying high ability. Easy assumptions about the nature of ability are now dangerous foundations on which to build an educational system. To prepare young people for life on the assumption that immutable permanence attaches to what may be only a transient phase of an evolving social and economic structure would be equally ill-advised. The pupils in the schools of today will be occupying key positions in the society of the 21st century. If what they learn now is to count, then we must bear in mind the rate of change. Our educational effort ought to be directed towards what lies ahead. We have only to recall the actual changes experienced in the last thirty years to realise how rapid the transformation of a society can be.

Until recently it has been accepted that our most imperative responsibility must be to extend the educational opportunities open to adolescents. In all European countries school leaving ages have been raised by law and very large voluntary increases in student populations have occurred. The aim has been that those with only average ability should be able to occupy positions of trust and responsibility for which an extended general education, as much as any specific skill, would best equip them.

We are only now beginning to explore the implications of the future as they affect the education of young children and the education of those who possess exceptional talent. Thus we have had in the 1970s a switch of national attention from the upper secondary and further education sectors of education towards the pre-school and primary sectors. It has been accompanied by a new and lively interest in the question with which this book deals—that of the education of children and young adults well above the average in ability. This seems a question to which increasing importance will be attached. I intend to argue that in the national interest generally and in order to make the best use of above average talent we need to think hard and straight about the present provisions for the age-range 12–15 in particular.

CHAPTER II

Ability and Equality

Egalitarian sentiments have exerted an influence on public
policy in most European countries ever since the French
Revolution. In Britain the direction taken has been towards a
more equitable distribution of opportunity to rise in the world.
Education became one of the keys to social mobility. It was
also increasingly significant because a society that grew in
administrative and technical complexity was forced to reward
more and more highly those who equipped themselves to take
on the more demanding roles. Education became an ordeal less
oppressive in itself and more clearly productive of tangible
prizes.

To most critical observers—and Matthew Arnold provides a
good example for our purpose because of his knowledge of
education—the society of a hundred years ago revealed three
distinct strata. Arnold looked at England in the year 1863 and
concluded that the ideal for the education of each of its classes
must necessarily be different. For the highest class the aim
should be "to give them those good things which their birth and
rearing are least likely to give them; to give them (besides mere
book-learning) the notion of a sort of republican fellowship,
the practice of a plain life in common, the habit of self-help.
To the middle-class the grand aim of education should be to
give largeness of soul and personal dignity; to the lower class,
feeling, gentleness, humanity."[1]

Arnold took it for granted that the role of the upper class was to govern, to take responsibility for other people's lives, to regulate the processes by which society cared for its members. The manifest weakness of aristocratic supremacy was the detachment of the aristocrats from the rest of society, their failure to understand or feel sympathy with the aspirations of the masses and their tendency to remain embedded in the eccentrically privileged conditions of their own life style. For them therefore school ought to form, in Arnold's words, 'a little world', a complete culture of its own in which precisely defined values were accepted and severe disciplines were observed. This is how Matthew Arnold had seen his father's Rugby and how thirty years later he seemed to see Eton when he wrote his three famous essays on what we would now call secondary education.

Arnold's hopes for the future rested in the belief that the outlook and abilities of the upper and middle classes could be fused. His supreme concern was not with the material prosperity of society (the acquisition of wealth he regarded as already too obsessive a concern of his Victorian contemporaries) but with its soul or culture, the standards it applied, the basic ideas which permeated its manner of life. The problem was that of first acquainting the middle ranges of society with "the best that has been thought and said"; and then of educating its members to discriminate between what was meretricious and what was of enduring worth. Public secondary schools for the middle class, once established, would drive out the wretched private schools, on which Arnold poured such scorn, because they pandered to all that was narrow and philistine in the mid-Victorian middle class. And in the long run all classes would benefit from the enlightened rule of a new middle class as well educated as was, in Arnold's opinion, their equivalent class in France or Switzerland.

In Arnold's view the social significance of education was very great. He believed that schools should serve national as well as personal needs. Sweetness and light, gentleness and humanity were not qualities on which he set a value simply because they corresponded with the kind of outlook and behaviour which he personally favoured. They were, he believed, basic, immutable foundations on which any decent society must necessarily be built. Book learning was of course an essential part of the educational process. From poetry, in particular, new generations were to draw that inspiration which religion had once given, but this could not be all. Arnold believed that the march of mankind 'on to the City of God' stood in need of moral as well as intellectual leadership. The direct example and continuous authority of such men as his father—"zealous, beneficent, firm", as he describes him in his famous poem on Rugby Chapel—must be elements in the training of youth as important as good learning.

Developments in English secondary education subsequent to Arnold, were to a notable extent the outcome of two men's work—Sadler and Morant, the first a scholar and the second an administrator. The pattern of school provision continued to reflect a stratified society, but the middle classes, at first particularly in the cities and elsewhere after the Education Act of 1902 and the new grant regulations of 1907, realised educational opportunities much nearer to Arnold's prescription. So did an increasing number of children who, after attending public elementary schools, obtained places in the reformed or newly created secondary schools. These schools steadily assumed a new purpose. From small-scale teaching establishments, designed to offer to fee-paying members of the middle class an education appropriate for their limited roles in a traditional society, some of them blossomed into institutions which provided high-powered academic teaching for the ablest pupils of all classes and a social distinction for those of lesser ability. Equal opportunity for all to obtain a secondary education there was not, but the claims of a child of marked ability to be educated beyond the level of the elementary school became finally established in England and Wales. The aim of enlightened Local Education Authorities in the 1930s was that all children who showed sufficient aptitude in an examination should be admitted to a secondary school. A few would be free scholars and for the rest fees were within the discretion of the Authority to fix.

After 1944 all secondary education in schools supported from public funds became free. It was not, however, possible to provide secondary schools for all at a stroke. It followed that entry was most coveted into those classes which were staffed and equipped to provide for advanced work in a range of academic subjects, and which, moreover in many cases embodied a considerable tradition of learning. Such schools had achieved a reputation based not only on the academic success of former pupils, but on their ready acceptance into promising positions in commerce and industry.

Two types of aided secondary school thus existed; those to which pupils who at least showed promise of achievement in academic studies were admitted, and those for children whose primary school performance did not appear to suggest any such possibility.

Here was a situation then in which ability of a kind was given recognition. It was indeed possible for a child with initial disadvantages of family poverty, and with no inheritance of educational attainments, to go forward to higher education and a position in society making demands on intellect and learning. Equality as a social aspiration clearly had two sides to it—one summed up in the famous phrase "*la carrière ouverte aux talents*". Ability should be the criterion by which to judge the suitability of individuals for responsible office and high rewards. But the notion of equality embraced also the building of an educational system to provide opportunities for all to *cultivate* their talents. And therefore, if the particular talent valued by society was the talent for performing the intellectual exercises necessary to pass examinations, then all should have an equal chance of acquiring it. Tests devised and administered by psychologists might of course be used as substitutes or supplements to teacher controlled examination. It is doubtful, however, whether anything other than suitability for the kind of extended education that the society provided was in fact measured by these tests, however ingenious they became.

There has always been a superficial attraction in the idea of a meritocracy. To be ruled by those whose conspicuous abilities have been reinforced by continuous testing to ensure that they possess and retain all the qualities required for the top-level jobs they do, sounds a good prospect. There will be times when the whole society is convinced that such should be its only course. In time of war it seems obvious that the highest intellectual talent should be employed in the planning of operations against the enemy. Trial and error—the error sometimes involving appalling loss of life—convinced us of its importance. Indeed, the Second World War carried forward a long way the techniques by which certain special abilities could be identified and human resources put to good effect. Air forces, for instance, rapidly learned that the personal attributes of an efficient captain of a bomber aircraft were not the same as those of a fighter pilot. The psychologist was trusted with a part in arriving at the proper distribution of service manpower. But to extrapolate from practices developed at that time, plans for precision instruments, designed to distribute the life chances of young children, has seemed to an increasing number of people to be an affront to human dignity, both an unfair and socially damaging thing to do. Procedures which received general consent when applied to adults were not found tolerable when applied to children. That British eccentricity—a national competitive examination for children of 11—was initiated nowhere else in Europe and can hardly now be found even in its country of origin.

It is worth looking for a moment at the place of élites in a democracy. Whatever the nature of the society, those who possess the keenest inclination to learn are marked off from the rest. It may be simply that by their own choice they live a different life—that they become hermits or group themselves together in self-contained communities. In that event they may be tolerated by society or they may be suppressed: if on the other hand they choose to become functional members of their society, accepting it on its own terms, then the probability is that they will constitute some kind of special group, a minority;

perhaps, to use Arnold Toynbee's term, a creative minority. In this phrase one might describe those minority groups which provide society with services that are recognised by all. No resentment is felt against the privileges, emoluments and powers which such groups may acquire as long as their members perform for society as a whole those services which they alone can give. Not only lawyers and doctors, but popular entertainers of various types, constitute groups of this kind in the contemporary world.

Toynbee, however, distinguishes between creative minorities and what he calls "dominant" minorities.[2] Most other writers use the terms "ruling class" or "political elite" to indicate those minority groups who occupy the commanding heights in the structure of a society. Certainly there is a difference between those elite groups whose social activities are restricted to the performance of a function for which their abilities demonstrably qualify them, and other groups, merchant bankers, or trade union leaders, whose scope for power extends more widely. These are the potential constituents of a *dominant* minority: royal nominees, or party officials nominated by a Chairman, Chief Secretary, Field Marshal, Führer or Duce have run most states in modern history.

Political democracies such as our own are distinguished from totalitarian regimes because the government is accountable to an electorate, and limitations are imposed on its day-to-day exercise of power. These restrictive influences are expressions of the cultural unity of our society which may be seen in such things as general respect for the rule of law as much as in any written constitution. In a democracy it is believed that the seats of power should be open to all, but that those who occupy them should be exposed to the criticism of their fellow citizens and answerable in the end to the same public opinion that elected them to power. Such people inevitably form an elite. They can only be a minority but the just demands of egalitarianism can be satisfied provided that the nature of their power remains that of the creative and not the dominant minority.

From this analysis it might well be deduced that society

should aim at an educational system with the capacity to train-up a creative minority. And indeed this is exactly what most societies have aspired to do, but the channelling of effort has now to be very carefully considered. Intellectual ability should clearly constitute one of the qualifying conditions for those forming part of the creative minority. But what is intellectual ability, how can it be discovered, how can its application to socially valuable objectives be assured? None of these are easy questions to answer. Nor can intellectual ability alone be taken as a sure token of eligibility for leadership. If the elite which governs, subject to democratic recall, is really to become a creative minority, then creative qualities would seem as desirable in its members as intellectual ones. If the aim is to provide an educational system of the kind suggested above, then a whole new set of considerations is raised—what to do about creativity, what to do about moral responsibility, what to do about codes of ethics, for instance.

The ideal of equality cannot easily be reconciled for purposes of educational policy with two vital considerations. One is that differences in the ability to learn are among the facts of life; differences in the will to learn, arising from whatever cause, are no less certain. Plain common sense, and indeed realisation of the full concept of equality, support the gifted child's right to go forward educationally to the limit of his or her capacity. The other is that the very process of remedying injustice by removing inequalities of opportunity (insofar as this is possible) may introduce an alien, possibly a cancerous element, into education, and thus seriously distort its true aims.

Michael Young's satirical fantasy *The Rise of the Meritocracy* develops this point. He starts from the assumption that the principal injustice which the pursuit of equality sets out to remedy is the denial to intelligent members of the working class of their due in education and the rewards which education brings. Once this has been removed, by a massive extension of testing and examination, so that every individual's opportunity to ascend the ladder is vouched for by objective measures of ability, then all sense of grievance will be removed. Only an idealistic minority interprets the idea of equality as extending to equality of income. Sustained objection to inequality of reward would be negligible once inequality of opportunity and great differences of inherited wealth have been removed.

The Rise of the Meritocracy purports to be the work of a typical meritocrat, a former student, he tells us, of that most highly selective institution, the Manchester Grammar School. In his eyes a permanent social order has been created by the year 2034 of so patently fair and efficient a character that no reasonable man or woman can have cause to challenge it. Nevertheless he has to record, and the purpose of his essay is to explain, the rise of a Populist Movement, threatening all that he holds sacred and of proven worth. In this movement dissidents of all kinds are united. The servant who feels in his bones that he should be a master, the N.C.O. who has the certainty that he ought to be an officer, the technician who cannot see why his claim to become a technologist is denied by the test procedures universally adopted and applied.

With prophetic insight Young places the leadership of the unrest in the hands of women of outstanding ability. The women's leaders, he tells us, Urania O'Connor, Lady Avocet and the Countess of Perth, did not create the movement, but they seized their historic opportunity and used their conspicuous and unused ability to give it purpose and direction. This is what is done by all entitled to call themselves statesmen. Today one of the political parties is led by a woman, and one outstanding candidate for the future leadership of the other is also a woman. There is some reason to suppose that without distinction of party the ablest and most talented males prefer positions of responsibility in finance, industry, the trade unions or research to careers in politics. This was the situation forecast by Shaw in *The Apple Cart*.

In modern Britain the 11 + examination, as a system of testing attainment and ability, provided in the 1950s the high water mark of educational selection by merit. On the foundation of this general test those who had the capacity to benefit from a serious academic type of teaching and thus eventually to fill the

more demanding roles in society were to be separated from the
rest. The schools to which they were allotted were to have special
facilities, special styles of teaching and more highly qualified
teachers. They were the Grammar Schools and the Girls' High
Schools. Their products ought, if things went according to plan,
to gain entry to higher education, to secure membership of
professional bodies, or in some other way to derive profit from
their educational advantages.

Developing countries, it seems, are almost bound to follow
this classic pattern. For the very idea of modern development
implies the application of trained intelligence to technical and
administrative problems. Such application can only be brought
about by the agency of specialists. Developing societies have
thus to acquire, cultivate and deploy to the best advantage an
ever increasing number of trained experts, functionaries or
bureaucrats with adequate qualification for their role. The
function of education is the supply of a flow of individuals with
these qualifications and therefore, unless scarce resources are
to be wasted, selection and examination processes will dominate
the education system. Ability must always take precedence over
equality.

It was against the British background of achievement in the
selection of talent that Young elaborated his projection into the
future.[3] He observed the emergence of processes by which
opportunity was more equitably distributed and then showed
how its further development could lead to the creation of a rigid
totalitarian orthodoxy in which the State power policed the
family, controlled parental influences and drafted children into
the education and occupation appropriate to their measured
ability.

As Young had forecast the women and the rejected rose
against these model tactics in social engineering. In fact the
Revolt of the Mums, as a Roman Catholic Archbishop described
it, overthrew the tyranny of the 11+ in association with the
largely feminine rank and file membership of the National
Union of Teachers. Whether or not the system of selective
educational provision sustained or restricted the national

economy remained an open question. But a strong public feeling about the justice of the procedures slowly developed as the large age groups of the 1950s came under their sway. Educational opinion focused on the ill-effect of the selection tests on the curriculum and style of teaching in the primary schools. The 1954 Report on Early Leaving from Grammar Schools presented a disturbing picture of failure to ensure that the schools achieved the expected success with a substantial proportion of the pupils selected for them. The Crowther Report was even more decisive in its rejection of the claims that classification of pupils could be relied on. The Spens Committee (1938) for instance had claimed that "with few exceptions it is possible at a very early age to predict with some degree of accuracy the ultimate levels of a child's intellectual powers."[4] The Crowther Report, twenty years later, expressed the view that any system of selection of pupils, however accurate a classification it may have provided when it was made, defaults on its reliability with the passage of time. "We cannot hope to avoid error by further refinements in the process of selection . . . with human beings no selection can be regarded as final."[5]

The injustice of the selective system was also manifest in the wide variation in the provision of grammar school places by local authorities, and in the great differences in size, equipment, staffing and standards of achievement among the secondary modern and technical school alternatives. In the mid-1960s rather more than 20% of the child population attended grammar schools at the age of 11, but some areas of Wales had more than twice this proportion in such schools, and some areas of England (West Ham for instance) had less than half. In some areas able children, attuned to the rhythm of teaching in their secondary modern school, achieved good results in C.S.E. or G.C.E. examinations; in some areas the ablest 11 + failures were transferred at a later age to grammar school. In England and Wales as a whole, however, those practices were rare. And yet the evidence accumulated that many kinds of ability were not fixed quantities, but fluctuated according to conditions and circumstances. The most important of these appeared to be the atmosphere of the home and the influence of the pupil's family. These factors seriously affected both the development of the quality measured by intelligence tests and the acquisition of those attitudes to learning which tend to make education a welcome and pleasurable process for the child.

Whether or not the child makes a good pupil in its first school is largely determined by family circumstances. Measured intelligence is not decisive at this stage. But measured intelligence does connect with family size; there is strong evidence that the younger children in a large family tend to have lower I.Qs than an only child or the elder children in a small family. Broadly one may say that values uppermost in the home life of some will correspond well with those of the school. In other cases the culture of the home and the culture of the school will be in conflict. This is often attributed to life style differences between the skilled and semiskilled and the unskilled manual workers who tend to have the lowest incomes and the largest families. But of course it is not only family size and family poverty which may adversely affect children's educational progress. A host of other factors may stimulate or depress the child's response to school. The emotional and material security of the child's home is perhaps the most important. The encouragement of parents may be vital and above all perhaps an assurance to the child that his success in learning gives pleasure to those he loves.

The thing that has made a strictly selective provision of education in this country—and in other countries—unacceptable to public opinion is not only the demand for greater social equality, but also some general conclusions about the way children learn and the distribution of the ability to profit from teaching. And these views, which have influenced educational reform all over Europe, are derived from protracted observation of children themselves. The ability of children to profit from school is not constant. Response to learning opportunity ebbs and flows in accordance with an immense variety of formative influences, some human and some material.

The richly varied talents of children are not measurable by

a single test of so-called general intelligence. Giftedness has many facets and talented children are not all talented in precisely the same way. The needs of children and the advantages they gain from school are not all of an intellectual, academic kind. Social and moral education, the achievement of mental and emotional stability, of respect for the rights of others, of a capacity to secure control over one's own impulses —all these are among the many expectations which parents may reasonably entertain about what schooling can do.

Shop assistants in the small country towns of my youth took one's money, packed it into a small cylinder, pulled a lever and fired the package along overhead wires so that, travelling like a supercharged cable car, it arrived in some secret destination at the back of the establishment. Time passed. The mechanism was again triggered off. The cylinder, returned to the assistant, was unpacked to yield up a receipt and the coins due in change. This whole operation, speedy, efficient and wonderful to behold, seems to provide some people with an image for the process of education. It would be a relief to parents and of obvious benefit to society if the young *could* be processed in this way, packed up and posted off to suitable programmes of instruction, from which they would in due course be returned to that place in society for which their education would precisely have fitted them.

To use such a model for education today would be disastrous. By definition education must be a protracted series of events. There is no reason to suppose that it is a continuous process; rather it seems to move by fits and starts and, as with biological developments, critical periods may well be involved. From the angle of the individual a truer image is to be seen in all the myths that centre on a journey or quest undertaken in order to gain something from life which would be unattainable by merely staying at home. In countless stories, originating all over the world, a young man sets forth on such a journey. Success depends on keeping calm, being surprised at nothing, intuitively adjusting oneself to the situations encountered, or simply on the virtues of compassion, courage and persistence. Some lines

C

from W. H. Auden's poem "The Quest" bring out this point.

> Suppose he had listened to the erudite committee,
> He would have found only where not to look;
> Suppose his terrier when he whistled had obeyed,
> It would not have unearthed the buried city;
> Suppose he had dismissed the careless maid,
> The cryptogram would not have fluttered from the book.

So it is on the journey into understanding and maturity which education represents.

Even from the angle of society the crude image of packaging and processing is no longer a satisfactory educational model. The world is changing at such a pace and in so many ways that confident assertions that education should serve this or that particular purpose are fallible and therefore futile. As a production technique the classical division of labour is rapidly losing its validity. Modern technology tends towards demand not for the "hand" but for the technician, able to supervise mechanised chains of production. An all-round ability including that of achieving reasonable working relations with those different from oneself in role and background becomes steadily more important. It is not only types of employment but the responsibilities of citizenship in its widest sense that have become immensely more complex.

All the trends of our times seem to suggest a future largely unpredictable but already to be seen as making new and different demands on the resources that we devote to education. Economic determinants have revolutionised social conditions and class structures in the past, and in consequence educational aims and processes have changed. They are changing now with an unprecedented rapidity. The evolution of a more egalitarian, less type-cast society in which adaptability and creative talent are valued at all levels is apparent all over Europe. Much of what has to be taught will be more open-ended, less the product of a stable culture and more in accordance with the shifting economic, social and cultural currents of our age. These developments increasingly require that the individual should adapt himself to change, supplementing his previous education and re-training in new skills. Such unfamiliar demands will impose considerable strain. Many individuals will experience difficulty in coming to terms with new value systems and behaviour patterns.

In these circumstances the influence within a society of those with deeper insights, more vivid powers of self-expression, more pronounced capacity and inclination to lead opinion will be of the utmost importance. Such people will necessarily be drawn from amongst those in a society identified by performance as its ablest or most gifted members. Some will have profited from extended formal education and other have continued to educate themselves. The common element of the education in either case will not be the acquisition of any particular skill, or concentration on restricted fields of learning. This is demonstrable as much in the case of science and technology as in the humanities.

Sir Peter Medawar removed some dangerous illusions in his essay entitled: *The Conceptions of Science.* "As to scientists becoming ever narrower and more specialised: the opposite is the case . . . At the turn of the century an embryologist could still peer down a microscope into a little world of his own. Today he cannot hope to make head or tail of development unless he draws evidence from bacteriology, protozoology and microbiology generally . . . Isolation is over; we all depend on each other and sustain each other."[6]

If then it is claimed that the education of the ablest members of society is an aim of the utmost importance, which is today receiving too little attention, then there is need for a fresh look at the principles on which that education will rest. In what J. K. Galbraith has mockingly called the ceremonial literature of education words like "heritage", "civilisation", "culture", are in constant use. They point to agreed, though not always clearly visualised, targets for the efforts of teachers. Their ablest pupils are those they see as potentially the greatest contributors to the culture of the future. For, as the word itself makes apparent, culture must always be concerned with growth and improvement. The most valued members of a society are not those who rule, but those who by thought and deed refine the quality of its culture and extend the influence of its best features. Able children, in whom resides the possibility of achieving such ends, have to learn on the one hand a broad humanistic understanding of those aspects of the common culture—scientific, technological or artistic—to which they are most drawn, and on the other hand to govern their own beings, so that passions, prejudices and flaws of character are not permitted to obstruct their path.

Today it seems that the presence of great differences in ability and its causation produces the conditions of a storm. We are swept by cross-currents of thought about educational policy and planning. But nothing new has arisen to weaken the case for close attention to what we do for our most able young people. Their claims on social as well as personal grounds are still strong.

CHAPTER III

The Nature of Talent

In adult society the gifted are readily distinguished as those whose abilities have rendered them outstanding among their fellows because of some positive achievement or public performance. This cannot be the position where children are concerned. It is only to a limited degree that the ability of children can be demonstrated in action. In any case the important thing about children is their potential, not their present performance. A child who reads at the age of two and plays the violin at five is outstanding among children but not of any special value to society. But if the child becomes a young woman who speaks five languages, or a young man who draws three thousand people to hear him play, then there can be no mistaking the demonstration of special gifts. The problem with many gifted children is that they are difficult to recognise as such. Of course there are adults who become unhappy, even neurotic, because it appears to them that their exceptional talents are not recognised, but exceptional ability is objectively defined with the greatest clarity in all societies. It is the demonstration of a distinctively high level of performance in a sphere of activity on which society places a value.

Exceptional ability in individuals is thus delimited by social determinants. It is the nature and the situation of the society which places a value on the unusual attributes of its members. In a primitive society which maintains itself by hunting unusual

potential.

keenness of sight or swiftness of foot would be regarded as
exceptionally important gifts. Neither of these attributes is seen
in that light today. Nevertheless in a modern advanced economy
artistic and athletic talent can be very highly valued.

Exceptional ability takes many forms. Its recognition depends on social factors and it is for practical purposes relative,
not absolute. In other words it is a concept which implies the
existence of a scale. The only way of establishing a claim to a
special gift is one's ability to point to a great many other people
manifestly less gifted in that respect than oneself. It is because
this conclusion is inescapable that in an egalitarian age there is
plenty of reluctance to consider the educational needs of gifted
children. The extent of the opposition to be overcome is
alarmingly clear from the opinions expressed by teachers and
the officers of Local Education Authorities in answer to questions
addressed to them in the course of the Schools Council's enquiry.
These are printed in the opening pages of Dr. Ogilvie's book[1]
which reports the results of the enquiry and we shall be bound
to refer to them again.

At this point it will be helpful to distinguish between two
aspects of ability. "I am personally extremely doubtful about the
wisdom of special provision for gifted children except . . . where
some particular skill is involved," wrote one of Dr. Ogilvie's
correspondents. The peculiar logic of this statement indicates
the difference between the concept of high general ability and
that of high ability of some limited and specific kind. The
Education Act of 1976 recognises only two special aptitudes
falling within this category—that for music and that for ballet.
Critics have been at pains to suggest that (as in the U.S.S.R.)
some other special talents sould be taken into account (including
that for mathematics). It is not easy to see why the Act should
discriminate in favour of two special talents and two only. In
fact there can hardly be any theoretical justification, especially
in a time of national economic weakness, for providing exceptional opportunities at public expense only to children with
these particular gifts. The explanation can only lie in the
existence of two or three specialist schools for music and ballet

which it would seem ridiculous either to close or to crab by cutting off pupils of promise. In the U.S.A., as well as in the U.S.S.R., specialised schools for those of high academic ability, or possessed of other specific talents, are to be found within the public educational structure. New York City, as was pointed out by James Conant when he was trying to level up the standards of American High Schools, actually maintained 33 such schools, including the celebrated Bronx High School of Science and the High School of Performing Arts.[2]

The Americans have found it particularly useful to distinguish between the all-round capacity to learn and the special aptitude that some children display for learning in the sphere of music or mathematics or for the acquisition of some practical skill. In consequence it has become customary to use the term "gifted" in respect of children whose abilities are of the first type and to employ "talented" as a descriptive term for those with special aptitudes of a limited kind. Of course there is a great deal of diversity within both categories. There is also wide variation in the degree of giftedness, as in the type and range of ability conveyed by the use of the word "talented".

There is not for instance just one way in which children may display a talent for music. Some are so clearly fascinated by it that they and their chosen instrument become virtually inseparable from an early age. In an instance noted by Dr. Ogilvie, on the other hand, a boy who had given no previous indication of talent was presented with a trumpet at the age of 8 and "could immediately pitch different open notes. Within a couple of days he was able to play two simple hymn tunes without any further guidance from the teacher." This instance reveals how impossible it is for the majority of teachers to judge a child's musical ability.

In mathematics there are equally numerous individual differences in the way exceptional talent can reveal itself. A child who sat down to calculate how many seconds he has to live until he reaches the age of 20 (one of Dr. Ogilvie's examples) is notable, but in school the same child may have shown a poor memory for rote learning, or even a total rejection of formal instruction

Adam - statemented :
strong potential in Maths.
not detected by T's :
given support work.

and no response to the idea of reading for information. In another of Ogilvie's examples a five-year-old attempted to count to a million, writing down the number he had reached every time he had to stop for a meal or bed. Later in the infant and junior school his writing of figures and ability to draw lines was not good and he made careless mistakes in calculation. Obviously there are various types of mathematical ability and a mathematical flair may not easily be recognised in a child's early years.

Children possessed of the special talents referred to above are frequently, but not necessarily invariably, found to have high intelligence quotients. That is to say that the tests normally employed are likely to place them amongst those who are above average in some kind of general all-round ability. These tests have as their purpose the relating of the mental abilities of an individual child to those of the average child of the same age. The intelligence quotient is simply a score which purports to show the ratio of mental age to chronological age. A child of ten with an I.Q. of 100 is of average ability. If he obtains a score of 110 he is said to have a mental age equivalent to that of a child of 11 and so one year in advance of his chronological age. Exactly the same technique could be used as a convenient means of indicating the relationship of a particular child to the average child in terms of reading ability, or indeed mathematical ability if satisfactory standardised tests of these abilities were employed. In many schools, records of the pupil's reading age are in fact maintained.

Francis Galton seems to have been the first, nearly 100 years ago, to develop the concept of a general intellectual capacity in children which must, he believed, be at the root of all intellectual growth or achievement. This quality of general or natural ability was held to be largely inherited in the same way as physical qualities were seen to be genetically transmitted. Such a view does not of course mean that bright children are born only to highly intelligent parents, or that backward children cannot occur in their families. Anomalies, which are very numerous, can be accounted for by the generally accepted Mendelian hypotheses about the chance combination of genes. Further-more it is accepted that mental ability, and for that matter personal qualities, are subject to much greater influence from the kind of upbringing and education that a child receives than is the case with physiological traits. Both heredity and environment are of significance and to many it seems a somewhat sterile pursuit to argue over the precise numerical weight to be attached to one or the other in determining intelligence.

The really important thing about the concept of general ability or intelligence is the extent to which it has proved useful to parents, teachers and administrators concerned over the education of individual children. Apart from securing him membership of Mensa, the possession of a high I.Q. is not by itself an asset to any man or woman; specific talent obviously is. Evidence of general ability may, however, be highly significant in determining the education which a child receives. The earliest of those who concerned themselves with finding and presenting such evidence were more concerned with children whose intellectual ability was exceptionally low. To identify those who were almost certain to gain little from normal methods of teaching in the ordinary schools was a useful as well as a humane objective. Children of feeble intelligence could at least be safe-guarded from treatment based on the supposition that they were lazy or wicked.

Tests of intelligence were thus first developed in Paris and subsequently taken up in California, New York and London. What was being investigated was the individual propensity for learning. There was no particular reason why this quality which was first thought of simply as general ability, as distinguished from a specific talent, should have been given the name intelligence. There was no proof that in creating tests designed to measure intellectual ability, the scientists were in fact achieving what they set out to do. Except for its obvious value in screening the backward child, there was no particular reason for educationists to attach importance to the new techniques of mental measurement. Bright children, the conspicuously talented, stood out by reason of their positive abilities, openly displayed.

If it became necessary to rank one above another this was easily done by questions testing attainment under any of the conventional subject heads under which school instruction was arranged. And yet the belief that general intelligence was ascertainable and important to investigate obtained a powerful hold in some quarters. It was never all-powerful. When all L.E.As were conducting 11+ examinations there were few, if any, which based their selection procedure on intelligence tests alone. The normal practice was to arrange that all those children competing for places in selective secondary schools should be examined in English and Arithmetic as well as having other primary school records and teachers' reports considered.

In certain circumstances a child's I.Q. may be a useful bit of information to have. It is on a par with its blood group in that respect. Another parallel is the child's weight. If there is reason to suppose that this differs at one extreme or the other from the mean, then it may be a significant factor in the child's health. Marginal differences in I.Q. should never be allowed to influence judgment about children's abilities, but the knowledge that one child has an I.Q. under 80 and another an I.Q. over 120 may be very useful information to possess.

The main concern which most parents experience over their children of school age is neither the question of their general ability in the sense used above, nor that of their special talents. The question foremost in their minds is whether their child has got what it takes to get on well in school. When young mothers discuss their children at the school gates, the first question asked is "How is he getting on?" The second is likely to be "What reading book is he on?" The answer to this, odd as it seems, will be expressed more often in numerical than in literary terms. Reading skills are recognised as the most significant of the school's contributions, but before any single skill is considered the general issue is raised. The ability of the child to accommodate to the conditions of school, to feel at home there, to respond positively to what is offered comes first. It is the general inclination of the individual towards those interests and pursuits for which a particular school stands which, if there are to be different types of secondary school, ought to decide the question of which is the most suitable. Parents by instinct and experience recognise this without recourse to the concept of general intelligence.

In any case the measurement of what is alleged to be general intelligence is only one way of approaching the question of exceptional ability. It became the one most widely used because the instruments for making such a measurement lay to hand. At first it was believed to be a trick that worked, regardless of the age of the child and little influenced by his upbringing or environment. Such beliefs are dying, if not dead. Jensen's research suggests that sufficient proteins in infancy can improve I.Q. by 18 points.

An alternative procedure could have been developed from the recognition by teachers that some children are outstanding not in only one or two of the activities and pursuits carried on in school, but in several if not in all of them. In whatever direction the work might take, a few children might be found proceeding further and faster than all the rest. Anyone who observes large numbers of children is likely to have noted from time to time individuals who seem to possess an outstanding general or all-round ability. Some of these will no doubt become the recognised polymaths of the future. There won't be many of them and they will not necessarily qualify for Mensa. Above all it seems to be the keenness of their curiosity and the voraciousness of their appetite for learning that distinguishes them. The observer is less aware of qualities of mind than he is of personality traits—their vigour, their independence, their capacity wholly to absorb themselves in what they do. This faculty of "exclusive concentration", as Philip Magnus calls it,[3] was particularly marked in Mr. Gladstone by all his contemporaries. The child-like characteristics which they noticed in him all his life seem principally revealed in his power of total absorption.

These then seem to be the factors which prompt teachers to recognise very bright children; they are seen as having potential not in one direction only, but in many. Everything arouses their curiosity and nothing presents itself as impenetrable.

There is no doubt, however, that teachers will vary in their recognition of young children as gifted in this all-round sense. Some may well distrust evidence of high ability which seems closely related to the special environmental advantages derived from a particular child's home background. The child with great verbal fluency, who achieved early reading skills as an outcome of parental support, may not be quite as distinctively bright as he seems. His ability should perhaps be judged in relation to the whole range of activities which primary education provides. It has been suggested that high general intelligence could usefully be tested along the various dimensions of the curriculum. The presumed object of the school is to develop skills or gifts in its pupils and these could be expressed in terms of subject areas. Language and Mathematics, as structured communication systems, forming one; physical activities, leading to control of bodily movement and skills in dance, mime and sport, as another. Once an idea of the different kinds of achievement at which the school aims has been formulated, then a set of parameters becomes available. The child of all-round high ability is simply the one whose specific talents are evident in all the fields of school activity.

The special abilities shown by children in school are naturally numerous. Those possessing high general intelligence are probably versatile, but many others will display conspicuous talent in one or two of their school pursuits. Such talent is normally spotted by the naked eye of parent or teacher at a comparatively early age. Pronounced manual and digital dexterity presents itself to view long before school is reached. Fluency in speech, a wide vocabulary, ease and grace of movement, a constructional sense, all these can be so vividly displayed by young children that exceptional ability in language, in physical pursuits, or in mechanical aptitude may be presumed.

Another set of aptitudes which adult observers are bound to notice at an early age are those personality traits which give promise of future achievement. Curiosity, imagination and persistence provide examples. Then there are the mental powers which can be seen in operation. Memory is certainly one; an insistence on accuracy and exactness may be displayed; keenness of observation and the rudiments of logical thinking may be noted. All these attributes can reveal themselves quite early in a child's life.

In Hitchfield's study of able children and their families the parents were asked whether they considered their children, who had been selected for study, to be highly intelligent or gifted. Not all the parents of these children accepted the proposition that their offspring were exceptional, but most found it easier to indicate special talent than they did high intelligence. Some abilities of a general nature, however, were repeatedly mentioned. Powers of memory were among the most frequently indicated possessions of the gifted. Concentration followed closely as an indication of intellectual ability. The capacity to display initiative and find out things by themselves and by their own endeavours was another quality which impressed parents. Patience is occasionally mentioned as something supplementing this. Accuracy is also cited, as in an instance where a mother said of her daughter, "Everything has just got to be the way she wants it. If there is a slight error, it has to be scrapped and started again."[4]

Ogilvie's results from questioning teachers are also of interest. Those assisting his survey were asked to indicate the characteristics of the gifted children they knew. The percentage of respondents marking particular items in the list presented to them was as follows:

Intense curiosity	— 65%
Wide vocabulary	— 65%
Imaginative writing	— 56%
Rapid reading	— 48%
Extraordinary initiative	— 48%
Unusual and original behaviour	— 45%
Extraordinary perseverance	— 36%
Extreme independence	— 36%
Exasperation in the face of constraint	— 28%

Ogilvie makes a most important comment on these results. "The fact that no one characteristic received more than a 65%

'recognition take' suggests that the vast majority of teachers do not anticipate that giftedness reveals itself invariably in one type of behaviour. 'Giftedness' is a complex concept, and it is perhaps not surprising to find that teachers expect it to be displayed in complex combinations of behaviours rather than in any simple form."

In general personality factors, the early acquisition of skills and the possession of certain traits of character are mixed up together, not evenly distributed.

That imaginative writing and divergent behaviour should appear so high in the list must open our eyes to another area that needs to be investigated before the full nature of exceptional ability can be described. The adjectives "imaginative", "original" and "creative" are used about certain children by teachers and parents—less often by parents—in these surveys. They seem to denote aspects of high ability in the children concerned which are not special gifts nor aptitudes, nor covered by the concept of general intelligence. This has long been understood, but it is only recently that psychologists have made serious attempts to study the phenomenon of creativity and to try to measure the creative imagination of individual children. Much controversy has flowed around this development. Some psychologists still appear to be confident that creative thinking can only be an intellectual process and therefore an outcome of general intelligence. Others disagree—MacKinnon very positively indeed. "It is just not true that the more intelligent person is necessarily the more creative one."[5] Common observation seems to make it equally apparent that highly creative individuals may lack a decent measure of that native intelligence which belongs to all humanity.

The Victorians talked a lot about men of genius. They did not mean polymaths, but rather the most active agents in the progress of the human race. The 19th century was an era of confidence. T. H. Huxley was more cautious than many other of its great figures, but he did claim that science enabled one to see "in man's long progress through the past, a reasonable ground of faith in his attainment of a nobler future." In the later years of the century it was not so much vigorous Christians, like Thomas Arnold, to whom reference was made in the last chapter, but imperious men of action in the fields of politics, science, industry and exploration, who became the conspicuous leaders in the "march of mankind", to repeat Matthew Arnold's phrase. The most distinctive attribute perceived by Galton in the great men of history was what he described as "originality of conception". The ablest children may therefore be those in whom creative powers reveal themselves through the uses they make of their imagination. Ability may be revealed in the display of such powers, even more than in that quality of general intelligence which the long-established tests set out to measure.

High ability, we may conclude, is not on closer examination a simple unitary affair, but rather something produced by the build-up of various qualities. It is a many-sided phenomenon, not only because special talent takes many forms, but because all-round ability of a high order can be shown to derive from several kinds of mental power, and from personality factors. If ability is regarded only in terms of aptitude for learning, then a number of different kinds of aptitude can be distinguished. A special measure of linguistic, scientific, mechanical or artistic talent may be remarked in quite young children. There is evidence for believing that one general factor—that of above average intelligence—is to be found in all high achievement. On the other hand, the long practised procedures for measuring this factor have been recently under critical fire. Imagination and originality in the eyes of many are qualities different in kind from intelligence as measured by the standardised tests. Recognition of ability demands that these qualities are also taken into account.

There is another way of looking at the question we have been asking. For practical purposes, it could be held, our concern is not with high ability as such, whatever that may be, but with high achievement. Clearly that is something which depends at least as much on extrinsic factors as it does on any form of innate capacity. It depends on physical nourishment, access to opportunities, support and sympathy of the appropriate kind,

delivered at the right moment. Above all it appears that motivation and the will to achieve underwrite the effort of those who
put talent to the greatest use. No one can be sure how these drives
are aroused. In all the evidence that has been collected about
high achievers there is constant reference to patience, persistence,
curiosity and other personal qualities of that kind. Liam
Hudson[6] in some very suggestive speculation on originality of
conception points to self-confidence, fighting spirit and readiness
to take risks, also to the possession of a rebellious nature, as
important characteristics of the original thinker, the man whose
quite exceptional abilities are realised in the work of his life. He
quotes a statement of Freud's which is perhaps a good point at
which to leave this question for the moment.

". . . I am not really a man of science, not an observer, not
an experimenter, and not a thinker. I am nothing but by
temperament a *conquistador*—an adventurer, if you want to
translate the word—with the curiosity, the boldness, and the
tenacity that belong to that type of being."

CHAPTER IV

The Identification of Talent

Parents, as the politicians are now fully aware, have become increasingly interested and concerned about the teaching in the schools which their children attend. They are also better informed. Many are more aware of ideas about education because they have received more of it than their own parents did, and because the media—radio and television in particular—now give much more time and attention to educational questions than was the case a single generation ago. There has always been an audience of adult eavesdroppers for the schools' programmes; in recent years discussion programmes, aimed at helping parents to grasp some educational principles and learn a little about child development, have grown in number. Primary schools have become more open places in which an increasing number of adults who are not professional teachers have a part to play. In some instances parents of the ablest children may take the lead in the organisation of parental support for the school and interest in its plans and programmes. In others, the research of Miss Hitchfield seems to suggest, parents of the truly able are so anxious not to appear boastful or superior ("cocky" or "big-headed" were the terms generally used) that they tend rather to withdraw from school contacts. Some fear may well attach to the idea that one has a child in any way abnormal, and high ability in children is often associated in people's minds with eccentricity or truculence.

D

Dr. Bridges believes that the parents of gifted children are often in serious doubt about how to deal with them and that their problems may be greatest even before the children enter their first school. In summing up his eight years of experimental work[1] with children of high ability he concludes that their needs are often ignored or if recognised, not adequately provided for, with the result that their attitudes to learning are affected and their potential is not realised.

No very exact studies have been made, but there is reason to believe that the high abilities of some children—particularly those who belong to families in which there is little or no previous experience of special talent—can remain unrecognised. At home this may be due to ignorance, indifference to the educational progress of the children or to the stresses of circumstances affecting the family as a whole. At school the same possibility may be present. Teachers may fail to recognise high ability; they may shrink, perhaps on principle, from exerting any special effort on behalf of the children who are obviously bright. More often the pressure of managing a large class is too great to allow them the energy for coping effectively with the most able. "In this area"[1] wrote one of Dr. Ogilvie's L.E.A. respondents, "teachers' study groups are not likely to be welcome in order to study gifted children . . . teachers would feel that they had other more pressing problems." Many parents might say the same, but this could hardly be a wise stance for a far-seeing central government authority to take up. It has been argued already that high ability in individuals is of the greatest importance to national welfare. It is also demonstrable that effective educational help can be given to backward and handicapped children only when they are identified as individuals and the nature of their handicap is fully understood. Both to study their needs and to educate them, it is necessary to establish as objectively as possible which the "gifted" children are. How is this to be done?

It might be suggested that those who know the children best will have little difficulty in recognising their special talent. In many cases—especially those in which a single, specific aptitude or skill is displayed—this is certainly borne out in practice. But there is evidence, to which we have already referred, that parents can be uncertain and indeed quite mistaken about the degree and range of ability their children possess. Teachers' identification of the gifted may in favourable circumstances be much more reliable. Their estimates of the intellectual ability of children below the age of nine, however, are bound to be influenced by the children's powers of verbal communication and probably by other extraneous factors. When teachers move quickly from one school to another, and within the English system in which a teacher receives a fresh group of children each year, children may not be known to their teachers for any great length of time. Those well-adjusted to school and in command of a vocabulary which enables them to speak up for themselves, will find no difficulty in having their talents recognised. But other children, equally able but socially insecure and linguistically as yet underdeveloped, may possess high abilities which only an acute and experienced teacher will notice.

However unattractive the prospect, it seems as much in the interest of gifted children as it is of those with learning difficulties that some objective measure of their ability should be attempted at as early an age as possible. Furthermore if our knowledge of the ablest children and their problems is to be enlarged then an acceptable means of identifying them so that they can be studied is obviously necessary. The real problem is how and when to do it.

The Plowden Report stated that there was a serious delay in the identification of slow-learning children. It contrasted the early concentration on overcoming the learning difficulties of physical handicapped children with the uncertainty and delay over taking special measures to deal with the slow-learners' case. In the past teachers have been reluctant, particularly in rural areas, to refer their very backward children for assessment. A gradual acceptance of the need for early recognition has been apparent in recent years, and a slow realisation that valuable expert help can be enlisted in identifying backward children, clarifying the causes of their difficulties and ameliorating their educational problems. We seem now to be at the beginning of a period in which the same kind of attention may be given to the ablest of our children. But first the reluctance to recognise the need and second the problems of definition and selection have to be overcome.

If the teaching they receive is to be suited to their abilities then obviously the identification of specially gifted children has to be made early. Where certain special talents are concerned this identification may reasonably be made by specialist teachers —music being a case in point. But if what distinguishes the child is a high general level of ability, then identification by some objective scale of measurement may be thought necessary. Central government money has been invested in the construction of an elaborate British Intelligence Scale and when this is ready it will no doubt be widely used.

Test results, however, merely string out children along a continuum. They do not, as Yehudi Menuhin might in respect of musical ability, choose for us those who are the gifted. To achieve that someone must select a point on the scale at which giftedness begins. An I.Q. between 110 and 120 was generally adopted as one of the criteria by which selection for grammar school education was made, but there were few grammar school teachers who regarded all their pupils as gifted. In a recent study[2] carried out by Professor Tempest, children with I.Qs above 130 were considered, and in America entry to one of the best-known special schools for gifted children, Hunter College Elementary School, is based on this figure as a minimum requirement.

The National Association for Gifted Children interests itself in the highest two or three per cent of the child population. Children with I.Qs of 125 and above contribute according to the estimate of the Plowden Report only 5% of the population. For practical purposes in education, Dr. Ogilvie's summary of teachers' opinion is perhaps the soundest thing to go by. Most of the teachers he consulted thought that I.Q. 130 provided a useful cut-off point for educational giftedness—"opinion focuses on a 2–6% band as marking off children who are likely, in most situations, to be sufficiently outstanding to warrant special consideration on that account."

In America the study of gifted children seems to have been unencumbered by prejudices arising from the grudging attitude expressed to Dr. Ogilvie by one of the Schools Council's subject Committees. "The fact that special consideration is being given to the gifted child seems to contradict the contemporary educational emphasis which is placed on such things as the integrated day, vertical grouping, non-streaming and non-selection." Professor Lewis Terman of Stanford University began his work, eventually published as *Mental and Physical Traits of a Thousand Gifted Children*, during the First World War. He had at the outset to select his material—a large sample of children in whom intellectual abilities were clearly apparent. To grade them he devised standardised tests of intelligence, a task he completed in 1916. The grand scale of Terman's longitudinal study, its uniqueness, and the credit awarded him by other psychologists for the excellence of the Stanford-Binet Intelligence Scale on which the project depended—caused his work to dominate investigation in this field for many years. Its value to educationists was limited, however, in two respects. First because his concept of "giftedness" was confined to general intelligence as indicated by capacity to produce a high score on his tests. No other evidence of ability was admissible at the point of selection, though various types of test were subsequently given to those selected. The second limitation lay in the fact that Terman's studies dealt with a sample of those children who would probably have constituted the top 0.38 of the population if all children had been tested. A massive programme of work, extending over many years as the progress of the original sample was reviewed through all its stages of development, had no great relevance for practising teachers when only one child in 300 could come within its scope. Terman's general title for the volumes he produced was *Genetic Studies of Genius*.[3] He was not using the word genius in the same sense that Galton had employed it many years earlier, but he was certainly confining himself to instances of exceptional rather than of merely high ability.

In the post-war era two American tests constructed to identify the existence of general intelligence were widely used in this country: The Terman-Merrill and the Weschler Intelligence Scale for Children. Both are individual tests normally administered by psychologists and involving face to face contact between the administrator and the subject being tested. Oral replies, written answers and the manipulation of solid forms may all be required. Group tests are of course far more economical to carry out. They can be set to large numbers of children working under identical conditions to a uniform time limit. They can be swiftly and objectively marked but they are not a means of obtaining precise information about individuals, nor in most people's opinion do they yield reliable results with children under the age of seven.

It was apparent early on in the history of mental measurement that intellectual ability had various dimensions or components, even though some factor, given the initial "g" by Spearman, might be thought common to all intellectual activity. Research, carried out by a number of people over many years, pursued the task of identifying the components of measured intelligence. Verbal reasoning ability on the one hand and spatial/mechanical ability on the other came to be accepted as two different common factors; such other possibilities as a capacity for logical thinking remained controversial.

Group intelligence tests have had their value as a means of screening a child population; confirming or calling in question subjective estimates of individual children's abilities. Individual tests enable psychologists to obtain information upon which their advice may be based and without which difficulties might arise over its acceptance. If early identification of high general ability in children, as opposed to specific talent for a particular pursuit, is desirable, as we have supposed, then it must be of some importance to know which are the means of identification most likely to be effective. The evidence from both sides of the Atlantic seems to suggest that group intelligence tests alone are not wholly reliable guides. Indeed it is a moot point today whether schools once free from an obligation to do so, will ever again find any useful purpose in them. Certainly no research project in which the selection of a group of able children was required would rely on the use of group intelligence tests.

One type of testing for ability is obviously valued by the teacher. She cannot but be concerned with the attainment of the children she teaches. Any objective measurement of this attainment will be of some value, but what serves the teacher best is a score for the level of a pupil's achievement measured against some standardised expectation of what children of the same age and apparently similar general ability could achieve. A backward reader for instance is generally regarded as a child who is below the average level of attainment for his age. But the question the teacher has to ask herself is whether this is due to the child's lack of ability or simply to his failure to profit from the teaching he has received. Our normal expectation would be that about 10% of all children would be retarded in this or another particular skill. Is the child with whom she is concerned in this category? If so we should not necessarily be doing the best to remedy the situation by spending more time on it or revising the method of teaching. We might do better by simply accepting that slower progress was to be expected. To try to push ahead faster would simply discourage the child by setting targets beyond his powers to achieve. If the purpose of testing children is to lie in changes of plan or procedure to remedy weaknesses disclosed, then it is a vital matter to know not only what these weaknesses are, but what is causing them.

Disabilities from which children may suffer in relation to reading are many; they can be physical, intellectual and psychological. Sight and hearing are factors that count, but in all cases the will or motivation to learn are manifestly important. Intellectual ability expressed in terms of mental age on the basis of intelligence tests is another important factor. Some objective estimate of this quality, whatever one chooses to call it, can be valuable when problems of individual progress arise. As the Bullock Committee's Report put it—"A high score on an intelligence test may supply useful information to a teacher who has underestimated a child's potential capacity."[4] There has, for instance, been considerable criticism of first school practice on the question of whether or not children are ready to start reading in the relatively formal conditions of the classroom. The Bullock Report deals with this question succinctly and with an authority that should put the somewhat emotional anxieties of some parents and some publicists to rest. In doing so the identification of the ablest children by some type of intelligence test is accepted as a helpful step. The argument of the Report is that teachers ought to help the children towards readiness to begin to read by means of a carefully thought out and prepared programme of activities and events, using as many pictorial and other materials as possible. The child's capacity to concentrate and the persistence with which he asks for help in reading then become the principal criteria by which to judge reading readiness. Very high intelligence will clearly affect the child's reactions just as much as very low intelligence. Thus, if the basic principle "that children should be given learning experiences that match their individual needs" is genuinely to be adopted, the early identification of the high ability is a necessary step in its realisation.

A child who has unusual aptitude or enthusiasm for books, mathematics, music or any other demanding pursuit, is as much deprived by indifference or neglect of his interests as would be a handicapped or backward child to whose weaknesses no attention was paid. In both instances the result of neglect is likely to be apathy at one extreme or rebellious frustration at the other.

As time went on and academic psychologists used it for research—particularly in America—more complex theories of the structure of the intellect were elaborated. Increasingly ingenious tests were devised to measure different types of thinking; detailed statistical analyses of their correlations were carried out. All this activity reflected a growing disillusion over the theoretical basis of the general intelligence test. This had proved valuable enough in identifying children in need of special attention because of their learning difficulties, but had not proved an adequate means of assessing intellectual ability in its widest sense. It failed to illuminate possible dimensions of intelligence and was partial in its operation. In 1959 J. P. Guilford in California published his model of intelligence, based on a factorial analysis of the various intellectual abilities which he claimed to be able to isolate. 130 separate factors emerged from this effort.[5]

In England this work and that of two other Americans J. W. Getzels and P. W. Jackson had some influence in the 1960s. The movement of attention it caused was away from the old theories of general intelligence as a static quality and towards an interest in the measurement of the actual output or productivity of thinking—the powers of reasoning and of memory, for instance, or the developing capacity of the mind to absorb (or learn) symbolic systems such as those used in language or mathematics. It became steadily clear that many intellectual processes were not being measured by existing tests. To track down and to construct new tests to identify them in individual children was therefore important. This country began its national effort to produce "a new British Intelligence Scale", which, perhaps in recognition of Manchester's nineteenth century reputation in the field of thinking, was located there. In America concentration centred on the identification of what was there called "creativity".

Guilford and other Americans wanted to obtain a better understanding of the type of thinking which was productive of original ideas. Existing evidence suggested that those who scored high on the intelligence scales then in use, would be capable of receiving instruction, amassing information and putting it to use. Terman's follow-up studies of his original (1921) sample showed that 90% entered college, large numbers did postgraduate research of one kind or another and published books or articles. The output of his sample in this direction was twenty to thirty times greater than what would have been found from a random sample of similar size. And yet there was some reason to believe that the type of thinking which produced original

ideas, new inventions, imaginative elaborations of concepts and
practical applications of existing theory was not identified by
the standardised intelligence test. The distinction drawn was
between the flexible exploratory, highly imaginative mind, and
the somewhat rigid, more conventional, less speculative thinking habits of those selected as the ablest individuals by the
normal tests.

Getzels and Jackson, who followed Guilford in their
researches, distinguished two types of child—the "High I.Qs"
and the "High Creatives"; these latter being the children who
scored well on so-called "creativity tests" and less well on
intelligence tests.[6] Liam Hudson called the two styles of reasoning, thus separated out, convergent thinking and divergent
thinking.

For purposes of educational treatment, as opposed to the
quest for information about the way our minds work, tests of
general intelligence had been shown to have their limitations.
The I.Q. might be the best single index of a child's ability we
had, but surely broader criteria of giftedness might be found.
And if they were, then we might secure a clearer, more reliable
image of the able child. "Creativity" tests were thus devised as
the means of identifying these powers of fluency, originality and
liveliness of mind which lay outside the competence of the
existing tests to pinpoint. It is of interest to note the nature of
these new tests. They are entertainingly described by Professor
Hudson who, while highly sceptical about the American concept
of "creativity" was so much attracted by their tests that he spent
several years administering them or variants of them to clever
schoolboys in this country. Eschewing the word "creativity"
he went in for open-ended writing and drawing games which
gave most of his subjects a good deal of pleasure, promoting
safe outlets for exhibitionist urges which the schools they
attended were no doubt endeavouring to suppress. At the
same time the patterns of thought and distinctive characteristics of able boys were considerably clarified by this work to
which we shall be referring again in the next chapter.

Hudson lays particular emphasis on the need, when studying

the phenomenon of high ability, to use various different lines of approach. He derived information about the intelligence of young people from interviews and the study of their auto-biographical writings and found it as valuable as that obtained from the type of test that can be scored. Consultations about a child's hobbies or interests, his enthusiasms, frustrations and disappointments provided insights into his intellectual develop-ment and into the nature of his abilities. [7]

Elizabeth Hitchfield's book *In Search of Promise* contains two highly illuminating chapters in which the able children whom she studied express their views on themselves, their school work, their teachers, their fellow pupils and on the character of the subjects which they learned. These were children aged 11 and some of their answers reveal extraordinary perception. "Science?" said one boy. "I'm not quite sure actually. It's about the earth—not the minerals, the substance of the world—the contents of the world, the things there are . . ." "I think mathematics is a form of calculating, working out things, puzzling them and trying to find out for yourself without other people helping you," said a girl. "Art," said a boy, "is the portrayal of moods by various tones and colours and designs." "Just trying to capture a scene—a scene that wouldn't stay for ever so you have to draw it to keep it there," is another recorded comment on art.

Many American experts in the 1960s came to believe that the kind of talent revealed by performance in open-ended tests of "creative" thinking were underrated and neglected in the educa-tional system of the United States. Sir Cyril Burt, however, died unconvinced by the claim that such abilities existed independ-ently of that general intellectual ability measured by the conven-tional tests of intelligence, which he had been using all his life.

Most of the work done on the concept of creativity has been with older children, but two Americans, M. A. Wallach and N. Kogan, studied the relationship between creativity and in-telligence in children of the age group which in England still took the 11 + selection tests. They published their results in 1965 and among them was at least one highly suggestive line of thought arising from the discrepancy, frequently found, between high intelligence and high creativity scores. Their tests of creativity revealed imaginative children who were highly gifted in their capacity for divergent thinking, but not of high intelligence according to conventional test results. Such children, they believed, tended to be "in angry conflict with themselves and their school environment. . beset by feelings of unworthiness and inadequacy." At the other extreme, children, high in intelligence but lacking in creativity, tended to attach exaggerated importance to their achievement in school. "Academic failure would be perceived by them as catastrophic so that they must continually strive for academic excellence in order to avoid the possibility of pain."[8]

This and other similar research has induced reflections on the possibility that some children might be achieving less in the primary school than they were capable of. Others might be driving themselves towards a level of performance in school tasks which was beyond what they could reasonably attain at this stage of development, and was reached only at the cost of considerable strain and anxiety. In the day to day life of a school the bright children are identified by their teachers as occasion arises. Judgements about the individual's power to take in his stride a new book or problem or learning programme are always being made. Some children are judged to be lazy and others are seen as over-anxious. From the ordinary processes of observation, as much as from specific research, a conclusion may be drawn that there are children who for some reason or another do not act up to their potential in school. They may have abilities that rate highly in intelligence tests, special aptitude tests or open-ended tests of imaginative thinking; but they do not realise their true potential in application to their school work as a whole. There will be more to say about these supposed under-achievers in later chapters. For the present the problem to consider is how they may be identified by their teachers and so assisted through their difficulties.

There seem to be two ways of approaching this question, though it must be emphasised that in many schools underachievement is not seen as a problem at all. In that event there is now ample evidence that able children from certain kinds of home are likely to suffer. Because their facility with words is less developed than that of children whose home background has promoted such facility, teachers will tend to undervalue their learning ability. Expectations of progress will be lower, the tasks set them will be less demanding. Shyness, absence of confidence, lack of self-assertion are factors which may well cause a teacher to mistake the real ability of a child. The whole object of Cyril Burt's work as educational psychologist with the London County Council from 1913 onwards was to find out which children had the ability to profit from academic secondary education regardless of the influence exerted by home background on their early educational attainment. Professor Husen in Sweden became interested in the same question in 1938. He followed up a sample of 1500 ten-year-old children, mapping out their test scores, school attainment and social background.[9] Thirty years later he concluded that the factor of early social setting or environment had been more highly predictive of success in later life than had their measured ability. Success in school seems most likely to depend on the decision of a succession of teachers that a child is bright. If that is broadly true, then there is a strong case for examining the possibility that some children may be under-achieving.

Another way of considering the gifted child whose attainment is less than might be expected was exemplified in Dr. Kellmer Pringle's study[10] of individual children whom she described as "able mis-fits". These children's difficulties were due to unhappy family relationships and attitudes on the one hand, and misjudged expectations of educational progress on the other. Some element of emotional disturbance was found in the majority of cases. In her sample of 103 children 84% were performing in school at a level two years or more below their mental age. Fewer than 50% of them had been judged by their teachers to possess good, or very good ability, though the average I.Q. was 134. The majority of parents in this study were in professional occupations.

misjudgement by teachers. → underachievement.

Miss Hitchfield's study of a group of gifted children who appeared to be under-achieving, produced far less disturbing results. The reason seems to be in the entirely different manner of selection. Her book records interviews with a dozen children with I.Qs ranging from 130 to 154. They were those placed not as one would have expected, at the top, but in the middle 40% of the age group on the rating of their teachers. Only one was a girl. The clearest impression that transpired was that they were children who tended to give their minds to one area of learning only. Some were competent enough in, for instance, oral ability, but really aroused only by the fascination of such pursuits as mental arithmetic. One particular boy possessed intensive interest and much knowledge of natural history, and country life, but was rated only average in general knowledge, reading and oral ability, and below average in mathematics. His concentration on his special interests had not been recognised as indicative of academic potential as it well might have been. But, as Miss Hitchfield points out, this was not the fault of the teachers, indeed it is possible to consider it not a fault at all, but a blessing. Her interview brought out that the parents wished, with some reason, to protect him from educational pressure and that he himself adopted the same attitude. ("I'm about average. I don't want to drop any lower, but I don't want to go too high either"). This boy seemed to have it in his power to achieve the things he would set his mind to. "Should anyone intervene in the judgment of a son who was hypersensitive and delicate, and in his element out of doors where his mind and body thrived?" asks Miss Hitchfield.[11]

strong influ' of home

One must conclude that serious underachievement is as likely, possibly more likely, to arise from personal and family circumstances affecting the child's performance than from anything the school is doing or failing to do. In Miss Hitchfield's opinion it would be mistaken to regard highly gifted children as a group at risk in the normal primary school. It would be a gross exaggeration in her view to relate them to either of the two groups of children who give urgent cause for concern, those who are handicapped by physical or emotional disabilities and those who come from severely impoverished home backgrounds.

The question of how children learn and how children think are obviously related very intimately. It is therefore essential that those concerned with children who show exceptional aptitude in learning or precociously developed powers of thought should know something of the work of Jean Piaget whose influence on English primary schools has been substantial. The mystery which Piaget has done so much to illuminate is that of the child's use of his experience to interpret all the various aspects of the world around him. He claims to have identified certain clearly marked stages of development in children's learning arising from their capacity to form concepts. This capacity of mind grows as the child achieves physical growth. At an early stage in development the child acquires the ability to use language, describing what he experiences and responding to verbal instructions. But his powers of reasoning remain limited. He is handicapped by not yet being able to distinguish clearly between external reality and the inner self, the thought in his mind and the thing thought of. In due course according to Piaget and his collaborators, the child's thinking will assimilate a form of systematic logic by which the world of objects can be understood. He will form concepts of number, time and area in a gradual process of acquiring schemata, as Piaget called them, plans and instruments by means of which learning takes place. At first the newly acquired element of logical thinking will operate only in the real world of concrete objects, actions and events. By the age of 11 or 12 the child's use of logical thinking should extend beyond the stage of concrete operations and advance towards the ordering of abstract concepts and the formation and testing of hypotheses. Over a long period a process goes on whereby the child accommodates his personal concepts of the world to conform to the objective realities that confront all of us.

The great contribution of Piaget has of course been the influence of his theories on educational strategy in the primary school. What the schools do must be appropriate to the stage of thinking reached by the child. Studies of the child have become the basis from which the principles of teaching are derived. The language, the planned purposes of the teacher and the learning materials provided are selected in accordance with the intellectual development of the children themselves. The intervention of the teacher should be aimed to provoke extension of activity or a stimulus to the demand for explanation of the results achieved.

In another direction Piaget's work seems to have potential importance which has been somewhat neglected. In his view the different styles of thinking which he identified stood in a hierarchical relationship to each other. He believed that the capacity for formal thinking on logical principles is reached only after previous stages have been passed. By providing, through experiments, profuse evidence of children's thinking, Piaget felt himself able to associate chronological age limits with his milestones of progress along the road to logical thinking. Naturally some children proceeded on their way faster than others; in other words a special aptitude for logical reasoning could be observed in some children. Positive evidence might be produced to show that they had passed out of Piaget's stage of mental operations in relation to concrete objects into that of formal operations of the mind in advance of the age at which this process of development normally began. Might this particular indication of high ability be even easier to observe than so-called "general" or so-called "creative" intelligence? It is certainly something more closely linked to the ordinary work of the school. High ability in logical thinking seems very much the same thing as high mathematical ability. In England during the early 1960s a considerable number of research studies were carried out on the lines of the experiments described by Piaget and his colleague Professor Inhelder. Some of this is described and summarised by J. B. Shields who was one who contributed to it.[12]

The study with which Shields was concerned in association with Professor Lovell, was of a group of gifted children, chosen from two cities in the north of England, aged between $8\frac{1}{2}$ and $11\frac{1}{2}$. On the Wechsler scale they had reached I.Q. scores of 140 or more. These children were tested and examined on their understanding of such mathematical concepts as volume, proportion, conservation, and were given certain Piagetian tests involving the use of balances, pendulums and chemicals. In general the results of this research supported Piaget's analysis of intellectual development. Most of the children tested were at the stage of concrete operational thinking. Only occasionally were they able to show ability for formal thinking. It might thus be supposed that the gifted child, as identified by teacher's judgment and by intelligence tests, was not similarly gifted in logical thinking. There is reason to think, however, that the children on whose responses Piaget's theories were built, tended to be of above average ability. Certainly other studies in England, to which Shields refers, supported his conclusion that the gifted child is likely to be at the same level of logical thinking as the average child three, four or five years older.

At this point it will be well to summarise. No one has discovered a single, satisfactory measure of giftedness in children. There are as many types of ability shown by children as there are talents distributed among adults. Unusually able children may be recognised at a very early age by parents or grandparents. Some may convince teachers in a nursery or primary school that they possess an unusual degree of talent for some specific activity or that their all-round ability is unusually high. Quite young children can display surprising powers of memory, command of language or imagination. It is unlikely that powers of reasoning will be revealed in the same degree at as early an age. It is when teachers begin to set up situations which call for the child to exercise powers of this kind that their existence or non-existence becomes apparent. How easily, for instance, does a child learn to follow complicated directions?

As the primary school programme becomes more teacher-directed, varying aptitudes for learning become plain. Achieving a mastery of specific skills comes easily to some pupils and presents baffling difficulty to others. Some of these difficulties are clearly related to the child's personality—a very shy child for instance will not reveal high verbal ability. Others are no doubt due to the general conditions that circumscribe the child's life. Genetic factors must certainly be involved, though this is less easy to establish unless tests are administered. There is the further question of a child's general attitude to school life and to the teacher of whom he sees most. Inspired by a desire to please, a young child can "over-achieve", in the sense that others, to whom earlier reference has been made, may be "under-achievers'.

Tests of general intelligence have been in use for many years. Recently educational psychologists have developed new tests based on the hypothesis that different aspects of ability can be identified and measured. General intelligence itself is now regarded as a quality comprising various components of which verbal ability and mechanical ingenuity are two. Other types of test have been devised to measure logical reasoning ability, and a faculty which Americans describe as "creativity", but which in our context is perhaps better described as originality or inventiveness. This is a quality in which it may be misleading to compare one child with another as such tests cannot be standardised. The information provided by the open-ended type of test is probably more important as a means of distinguishing styles of thought in individuals than for its predictive value, though in that, too, it may be significant for the counselling of older children and adolescents.

No two children are alike, and no two milieus in which children are raised will be identical. No certain future is predictable for any single child. It is not in society's interests that some fixed proportion of the child population should be designated as gifted and set apart from their fellows. Nevertheless children of high ability are no less precious than other children. They experience particular needs, among which is that of contact with others whose interests and abilities match their own. It is improbable that this need will be satisfied unless some organised effort is made on their behalf. If they are to be taught in such a way as to fulfil their needs, a careful deployment of teaching power will have to be exerted. Not all teachers either wish, or possess the power, to teach highly gifted pupils.

effectively. For all these reasons the usefulness of exploration into the nature and growth of intellectual and other types of high achievement in young children is indisputable.

CHAPTER V

What Bright Children Are Like

Those regarded by teachers as the bright children in their class are not necessarily the most talented, but they will possess a range of abilities and some distinguishing aspects of personality. Children with outstanding singular talents, as for music, art or physical activity, are not so likely to be pointed out as those who impress their teacher for a plurality of reasons. A positive attitude to school and therefore an enthusiastic response to the individual teacher's effort is the first factor in this. The child whose attitude to adults is fearless and confident and whose demeanour is willing and cheerful, falls naturally into the group which the teacher will, at first unconsciously, label as bright. After that preliminary judgment, the attention of the teacher tends to be absorbed by the child's progress in acquiring those cognitive skills to which time and effort must be devoted in school. Those pupils who readily succeed in the tasks set for them by adults, or who reveal an unusual determination to acquire for themselves a recognised skill, for instance that of reading, separate themselves from the rest in the teacher's mind. These are the bright children. But what are they really like? Can there be any physical or personal characteristic common to large numbers of them?

We have taken a quick look at the way evidence has been collected about gifted children, and how their performance in various directions has been compared with matching or control groups, composed of children not selected for high ability. The impression acquired is first that the mind of the conspicuously bright child seems to operate in such a way that skills are acquired remarkably quickly. This assumes that the motivation to learn is strong. The roots of motivation seem to lie in an eager curiosity, an urge to explore and pursue enquiries. A capacity to memorise and to think sequentially provides inspiration for learning; it accelerates the process and consolidates its results. But all this tells us nothing about the physical, and only a little about the temperamental, characteristics of the ablest children.

Terman, endeavouring to make his studies of the gifted as comprehensive as possible, was naturally interested in these questions. He began his research in the he-man, frontier-conscious conditions of American society in the Theodore Roosevelt era. Hence the child with intellectual leanings was popularly thought of as a weakling, timid and under-sized. Terman proved fairly convincingly that this was an illusion. On the statistical evidence of his studies, intellectually gifted children came out well above the average in health and strength. When in the 1940s G. W. Parkyn compared the measurements of a group of New Zealand children selected for high ability, its median height was two inches above the average for children of similar age.[1] Once, however, that the false stereotype of the precocious weakling had been removed, there was little more that survey research, based on aggregates and averages, could reveal. In any individual child there were clearly significant relationships between intellectual and physical development, but no useful generalisations about them seem to have emerged.

Research suggests that gifted children are physically above average, but this may simply be because in any given sample there is bound to be a disproportionate number who come from better off and smaller families. Whenever children have been selected on intelligence (including non-verbal) tests or on scholastic attainment, those whose fathers are classified in professional and other non-manual occupational groups are disproportionately numerous. In Terman's cohort of a thousand there were four times more than there would have been in a random sample. The physical growth of young people will obviously depend, in part at least, on standards of nutrition and child care. To some extent the same factors govern intellectual growth. There is no reason to think that children of good all-round ability will tend to be poor physical specimens, but of course this does not mean that all of them will be physically above average. Even to say that gifted children are on the whole of superior physique may only be another way of saying that most of them come from secure, well-organised, well-provided homes.

Research has concerned itself not only with the mental and physical, but with the moral and social make-up of gifted children. The commonest procedure has been that of obtaining from teachers a series of comments on different aspects of personality for each of those in the selected group. Teacher ratings of this kind seem to show, both in England and America, that the gifted children are those whom teachers would also pick out as the most honest, stable, prudent and trustworthy in their class, as well as the most lively and persistent. Such judgments are precisely what one would expect. A teacher is responsible for a group of children who depend on her for order, discipline and control as well as for new and interesting experiences. But to achieve these expectations the teacher herself depends on the active co-operation of children, particularly of those who emerge as the most active and adventurous in the group. It is a basic principle of classroom politics that such children should be wooed over to the teacher's side by giving them small responsibilities and privileges and by repeated small acts of encouragement. The child with whom the teacher can most readily communicate, who is ahead of the others in enterprise and understanding, and is therefore in some sense a leader to the rest, is inevitably the one rated highly for positive personality traits.

Outside the classroom the situation may be very different. Teacher expectations of the brightest children affect teacher estimates of character, and predispositions govern the opinions expressed. Parents may have quite different expectations. In the home another set of circumstances obtain. Conditioning factors will be less uniform and less predictable. The family may be large or small, affluent or impoverished, stable or insecure. The able child in a large family, in a remote rural area, with elderly parents or with no parents, is much less likely to be recognised for what he is. Human young develop slowly and with much individual disparity, but they do use their elders as models. In personal development there is no uniformity, no Piagetian stages, to be discovered.

Recent attempts to look closely at the characteristics of the most able children of primary school age have been of two kinds. Dr. Ogilvie's study of the teaching of gifted children, carried out for the Schools Council, brought substantial numbers within its scope, and collected the views of Local Education Authorities and of a large number of teachers. Some thirty schools were visited, and a number of children adjudged to possess outstanding ability were interviewed and asked to talk and write about themselves. Miss Hitchfield's work fell within the National Child Development study which examines the subsequent development of a cohort of children born in the week 3–9 March 1958. This is a representative group of all children selected only by date of birth. In 1965 a comprehensive survey of their development was carried out[2] and four years later, using the data thus available, a sub-group of those who were held to be "gifted" was drawn up. *In Search of Promise* is therefore an investigation of children aged 11 in which 238 children were interviewed and tested in a number of different ways. Extensive interviews were also carried out with their parents and the opinions of teachers were obtained.

Apart from such research studies the other main source of information about gifted children of this age in this country comes from those who have worked with selected groups under some particular arrangement made to provide special learning opportunities. Such programmes for small groups, often known as extended activities or enrichment programmes, generally have artistic and constructive as well as academic sides to them.

The regular contact between educational experts and the selected group of children and the experimental use of teaching materials and techniques appropriate for such children has produced some very penetrating insight. The most notable reported experimental programmes were those of Dr. Bridges at Brentwood College of Education. Another such project, more recently written up, was that carried out under the direction of Professor Tempest at Southport. Here in an ordinary school fifteen children with I.Qs over 130 were in the charge of a class teacher throughout a four-year period. Specialist assistance was provided in music, science and a modern foreign language, and a control group was set up, matched for intelligence, but following the normal primary programme. Other valuable information has been obtained from part-time classes arranged for selected groups of children in West Sussex, at the School of Education of Bristol University and in other areas.

Thus, since the Plowden Report, a great deal more knowledge of the characteristics and behaviour of able children at the primary stage of their education has been accumulated. Fifteen years ago the only places in which one would have found a high concentration of such children would have been in certain boys' preparatory schools, for instance, the Dragon School at Oxford or, at Cambridge, King's College Choir School. Today this might no longer be the case and that is a question with which a later chapter will deal.

Contemporary research into the nature and incidence of high ability in children has often combined individual case studies with the collection of generalised data from which statistically valid conclusions can be drawn. There is always a likelihood however that educational research effort will veer away from concern with the living person and concentrate on assembling such facts as readily yield themselves to statistical presentation. The problem is that of keeping simultaneously in mind children grouped into categories and children as infinitely variable as they actually are. It is because he is adept at this peculiar feat that Professor Hudson's book *Contrary Imaginations* is both enjoyable and illuminating. Hudson believes that the experimenter must be able to think of each member of his sample as an individual and he tells us that his own span of memory covers about 150 individuals. In writing up and reflecting on his research into the intellectual abilities of clever schoolboys, Hudson constantly stresses the individuality of his subjects. Their responses to his tests yield not merely statistics but amusing and often revealing insights into differences in style of thought and self-expression. We recognise these responses for what they are—messages communicated from one human being to another—and we admire Hudson's ingenuity in the technique of de-coding them.

Those who want to know more about children of high ability must watch them closely, ask them the right questions, offer them appropriately stimulating things to play with or activities to pursue. This is what Hudson does with fifth and sixth form pupils. It is not made clear how many of his subjects he interviewed, but an element of dialectic was incorporated in most of the tests he used, for instance that in which the subjects were asked for their comments on controversial and polemical statements. Autobiographies, another "test", appear to have provoked Hudson to one of his most important hypotheses. He believes that when we speak or write about ourselves we are simultaneously communicating with the outside world and defending ourselves against its onslaught. This defensive attitude is particularly marked in adolescents. "The impulse of self-protection" he suggests, "seems to have invaded so much of some boys' lives that ... they present less a Siegfried or Maginot Line, more a countryside laced with trenches."[3]

If one accepts that there are two types of clever boy—the convergent thinker who tends to have scientific interests, to do well in I.Q. tests, less well in verbal fluency or open-ended challenges to ingenuity, and the divergent thinker in whom such abilities are reversed—then it had been supposed that convergers would be more inhibited, less avid for experience and emotionally more on the defensive. The converger, it might seem, would be the more preoccupied with the defence mechanisms and the diverger with the expression of personal feelings.

Hudson argues, however, that the readiness with which the diverger engages in emotional display, is itself a form of defence, the counterpart to the converger's reluctance to be engaged. The diverger, and the equally self-protective converger, are embodiments of two different kinds of defensive systems.

In advancing these conclusions Hudson puts himself at variance with American research on the way the imagination operates. He is sceptical about the measurement of creative thinking abilities, a task on which Americans have entered with enthusiasm and some confidence. All he claims to know is that such bright boys do manifest evidence of originality, whether they be convergers or divergers.

Another warning from Hudson is worth heeding. In his later book *Frames of Mind*, even more than in his first book, he lays great stress on the complexity and diversification of the original, inventive impulses of human nature. He can see no reason why original work should not come from convergers and divergers alike. In summing-up, he observes "the convergence and divergence of an individual will determine not whether he is original but, if he is original, the field and the style in which his originality will manifest itself."

Whatever method or combination of methods is employed to identify a gifted child, he remains a unique individual. Much of the individual's personality lies submerged, outside the vision of the observer. But anyone with the interest and energy to perceive exceptional talent and particular kinds of promise in the personal qualities of a child can be helped by carrying certain characteristics in mind. If teachers are to be alerted and put in a position to help gifted children, then some kind of checklist, containing items indicating what they should look for, could provide a good starting point. Any such list would contain items related to specific skills and aptitudes, things indicative of high intellectual capacity and above all evidence of personality factors and attitude to life. These traits of character and distinctive qualities of temperament and outlook are probably the most important factors. They are the items which cannot readily be tested or measured, but which present themselves most forcefully to the alert observer.

It is interesting to compare two lists of behavioural characteristics, put forward as indicators of exceptional ability in young children. The differences between them simply emphasise the wide range of talent and extensive variation in personality traits that can be found. Gifted children, it can never be too often emphasised, differ widely from each other, and like all children, are so greatly influenced by the manner of their upbringing, the personalities and place in society of those nearest to them, that formal criteria for recognising high ability can only be of limited value. Dr. Ogilvie, to whose list of indicators, derived from the views expressed by teachers, we have previously referred, lays stress on this point. His list may usefully be contrasted with that drawn up by an educational psychologist, S. R. Laycock, which was reproduced in a D.E.S. pamphlet,[4] and has been used by teachers in West Sussex. Both lists agree on certain outstanding attributes which may be placed in two categories—acquired skills and features of personality. The following items appear near the head of both lists.

Aspects of Personality	*Skills*
Intellectual curiosity	Imaginative writing
Perseverance and concentration	Wide vocabulary
Initiative and originality	Observation and memory
Independence	Rapid reading
Imagination	Achievement in problem solving and reasoning.

Laycock's list contained no negative criteria, but in the teachers' list exasperation in the face of constraint, day-dreaming, rejection of school work and even delinquent behaviour were given by some teacher respondents as reliable indicators of giftedness. In the eyes of many teachers unusual and unorthodox behaviour seem to constitute a distinctive characteristic of the gifted. These perhaps are personality traits which particularly impress themselves on the adult in charge of a class of thirty children or more. In the eyes of the parents or the more detached observer of children, they are less noticeable. Miss Hitchfield's research comes out very firmly against the belief that the very able child is disaffected from school and even more strongly against the notion that he is more likely to be mal-adjusted than the average child. She found no evidence of excessive activity and restlessness among her sample of gifted children, though she noted in them an apparent tendency to worry about their performance and the degree to which their achievement was recognised by adults.

Although the teachers' list (Ogilvie) and the Laycock list broadly conform in regard to personality factors and the development of skills, there is another set of indicators men-tioned by Laycock, but almost certainly absent from the teachers' criteria. These are the personal interests of the subjects. Both lists agree that rapid reading is an indication, but Laycock develops this point more selectively. He believes not only that having several hobbies is a sign of giftedness, but that having reading interests which cover a wide range of subjects is sig-nificant. The will and capacity to make frequent and effective use of the library is another item on Laycock's list. It is sur-prising that hobbies and interests seemed relatively unimportant to teachers and that only speed, and not purpose, was instanced in connection with reading skills.

As part of the study made for the National Children's Bureau, children were invited for interview and asked to bring with them some evidence of their interests. Miss Hitchfield's description of the results of this overture is so revealing that it must be quoted in full.

"It may seem frivolous, but one could say that one could almost judge a child's ability by the weight of material he brought to the interview. Some children brought several bags and cases full of things and other members of the family joined in and helped in carrying these. There was never any difficulty with such children, they were eager to get into the room to start unpacking and talking about their things. The children who brought nothing were different in that it took longer to ease them into the situation and find some common ground to start them talking. Some, of course, had their reasons ready to offer—their models were too big or collection of rocks too heavy or their interest in a sport had not lent itself to producing anything that could be shown. The larger amounts of material certainly seemed to come with the most verbal children, many of whom could have spent the whole three hours just talking about their hobbies."[5]

Another predominant attribute of the ablest children clearly emerged from Miss Hitchfield's interviews and is quite extraordinarily absent from the lists to which we have referred. This is the apparently inexhaustible energy which some young children display. Such energy of course takes many different directions, but with gifted children a proportion will be expended in mental rather than physical effort. The ablest children seem to have it in their power to acquire the habits of mind to which J. S. Mill in his *Autobiography* attributed all that he had achieved in philosophy: "a habit of never accepting half solutions of difficulties as complete, never abandoning a puzzle, but again and again returning to it until it was cleaned up ... never thinking that I understood any part of a subject until I understood the whole." This is of course an account of acquired discipline working on a base of intense mental energy to achieve results. Miss Hitchfield's case studies of 11-year-olds contain examples where such development is predictable, and others where the same exuberant energies are present, but their future application is uncertain.

One example is a boy with an I.Q. 140 from an academic family of Indian origin. In answer to questions about what he liked at school he said, "I don't like English Grammar questions ... I like writing stories and things. I try at home but I never finish them, there is always something else to do." This boy's mother said of him, "He likes to be noticed by everyone else. He thinks he's good. He's joined a gym club. He's as keen as anything ... He said 'That's Monday evening and Tuesday evening. Now I've got to find something else for the other evenings'." Asked to write about himself when he had reached the age of 25, the boy produced this somewhat surprising effort:

"Last Thursday I went to a soccer match, and, as my home team lost, I got into a fight with one of the other team's supporters at the 'King's Head' pub. A copper had to go and break it up though. Saturday night, I planned to rob a big store with a couple of other men, but the police were tipped off by one of their rotten spies. They were ready for us, and now, in jail at Slogmoor prison, I find myself without a pub, barred windows, and hopeless food. Still I suppose it's better than having to buy food, new clothes, and not having to pay rent.

Still, though, come to think of it, I wish I never got mixed up in all these things."

As a contrasting case study there is that of another boy with an I.Q. of 140 who was regarded as a good all rounder with everything going well for him at school. His main hobby, pursued in partnership with three friends and extending over two years, had been the invention of a town with buildings, local government and banking services, its own currency and above all its elaborate transport system.

"It is 7.30 and the morning paper has arrived. I go out and collect it from the front door. I read it, get washed and dressed and have my breakfast. Time to go to work I walk across the road into the forecourt of the Wood Garage of Brumly Transport Group. Up the stairs and into my office, B.T.G. the largest transport group in the Brumley Area. They own both British Leyland and Daimler and to finish it off, Atlantean. Work on my desk. Extension of Trolleybus lines to Croft Avenue, scrapping of the 32 to Ington War Memorial and the 182 to Nottingham Lane. Start of the 109 to Upham. Oh dear, more and more. Then I am called out. 'One driver short on 23', says Jock, head inspector. At the same time my secretary calls and says 'Bill is here'. Bill is head of Maintenance and supplies. 'Do we need more Bus Stop stickers. We're running out.' Bill is always concerned with supplies. Anyway, the 23 to Five Ways is one driver short so I think I'll have a run or two until lunch break. Pete, Assistant Head, can take over while I'm out. The 23 BCB (Brumley Corporation Buses) Wood Garage, Rye Jersey Drive, Upton Corner Main Gate Old Road Terminus Main

Gate Army Offices Five Ways The Junction The Square and back the same way excluding the Extension to Old Road Terminus. On I go until Five Ways. Might as well stop for a drink. Finished Lunch break. After lunch, back to desk work. Should we have a pipeline supply of fuel from McNab fuel Ltd. Should we or not. I don't know? Its all up to fuelling and tanks department. More Work. It piles up. However it's now 5.30 and time for home. Across the fore court. Past the Brumley Air Bay. Past the Brumley Mono rail sheds. Over the car park and home. Time for dinner and relaxing in front of the TV. What's on 'This is BBCTV2 and now Spy Pie'. The music and then another day is nearly over[7]"

The will to be totally engaged, to lead the fullest possible life with prodigal expenditure of energy, seems to emerge as an outstanding characteristic of the highly gifted. Together with energy goes speed. Quickness of thought is in many cases as noticeable as curiosity or initiative. "The child seems to be ready with an answer almost before the question has been completed," observes Dr. Bridges.[6] An extremely important part of the conclusions he drew from the Brentwood experiment centred on this point. He found that some of the children selected as having very high ability worked extraordinarily fast and had not the patience to go back and read over their work. Many, on the other hand, seemed to have assumed a gentle pace of work conditioned by finding in their school experience that such a pace was perfectly acceptable. When such children found themselves amongst their intellectual peers they tended at first to be left behind by the leaders, but in a relatively short time they themselves adjusted the pace of their response, until that of the group as a whole became virtually uniform. In coaching a school football team exactly the same process is involved. The best school teams are not necessarily those with the highest individual talents, but those in which the pace at which their game is played has been speeded up by practice until it is uniformly high throughout the team.

Speed and energy, untempered by discretion, may of course lead the very able child into trouble. The teacher discussion

groups organised in connection with the Ogilvie study gave
consideration to behavioural characteristics of the gifted and
did not omit those that seemed negative or disquieting. Impatience, superciliousness, intolerance, obstinate perfectionism
were considered among the possibilities. Some teachers had
noted uneasy relationships between the bright child and the
others, perhaps accompanied by a preference for the company
of older children; in some a tendency to direct things and adopt
a dominating attitude, but in others humility about their
achievements and surprise that what seemed to them natural
should be regarded as exceptional. A number of factors were
suggested to account for the teachers' tendency to be wary of the
gifted child, whose questions might be "tiresome and difficult
to answer," whose interests might seem "unhealthy and precocious" and whose nature might be "self-centred, aggressive,
attention-seeking." Extreme forms of divergent non-conformist
behaviour are obviously difficult to accommodate in a large,
lively class. Often the association in this respect has been with
the inventive original child whose fierce blazes of energy might
at best seem to burn themselves out, wastefully from the
teacher's point of view, and at worst cause disruption or chaos
in the class. In such circumstances frustrated anger, petulant
exasperation, contempt for the feelings and failings of others,
may seem the noticeable characteristics of the very able child.

It is never possible to generalise and no good purpose is
served by anything other than close observation of the individual
and unprejudiced effort to understand aright. Gifted children
are at least as prone as others to emotional stress, to confusion
and self-doubt. Their defences may indeed be more difficult to
penetrate than those of the child with less intelligence and
sensitivity, but their stability and social relationships will be
just as much affected by family circumstances. The "handicap"
of brilliance and the "able misfit" are not parts of a mythology,
but elements of real experience as George Robb and Mia
Kellmer Pringle have clearly shown. Recent research, however,
has strengthened the belief that there is no *special* reason to
associate high ability with any physical, social or psychological

handicap. Most gifted children are all-rounders, healthy, lively, sociable and responsive. The misfits and the children at risk are those whose peculiar talents have not been recognised or understood, those for whom adults have shown themselves deficient in sympathy. Cinderella and the boy judged by his widowed mother to be lazy and good for nothing are prototypes. Folk lore repeatedly records instances of the gifted child misplaced or misunderstood and there is as much to be learned from such sources as there is from modern quantified research.

It is difficult, though not impossible, for parents of low intelligence, or in disturbed states of mind, to care properly for highly intelligent offspring. It is difficult for teachers, made anxious, or unfamiliar with the demands made by very bright children, to do what is best for them in school. Both need help.

CHAPTER VI

Keynes, Wells, Kipling

There is yet another way of trying to answer questions about the factors that affect the general development of the highly gifted. Much can be learned from a study of outstanding talent and its development in those whose lives, taken as a whole, were characterised by great achievements, widely recognised. In such individuals one can observe the influences of heredity and environment and of the way educational opportunities were fought for or seized upon, and of experiences critical in their effect on the training and application of their talents. There is of course a difference between genius and high ability, but there is also an overlap.

John Maynard Keynes was probably one of the three or four most gifted Englishmen of the 20th century. "Maynard with his varied gifts has captured the imagination of mankind and succeeded in influencing the course of history to a notable extent," wrote his biographer.[1] So large a claim hardly seems exaggerated even today. In countless articles on the measures taken by modern government, Keynesian economics is a familiar expression, composed in the same way as Herculean efforts, Socratic teaching or Fabian tactics.

Keynes was born in 1883 and so grew up and received his education in conditions very different from the present but it is on our times, rather than his own (he died in 1946) that his mark has been imprinted. His birthplace was the City of Cambridge;

his parents were an academic couple of intellectual distinction and with a strong sense of public duty. He was their eldest child. Expectations of high ability in the young Maynard must certainly have existed, but it was not until he was about eleven years old that clear signs of it began to emerge. His particular bent was for mathematics at which, it was recorded, he worked before breakfast in the months preceding his entry for an Eton scholarship. He was placed tenth in the election list of twenty, but was bracketed first in mathematics.

The years Keynes spent at Eton (1897–1902) were lived like a prince of the renaissance in the utterly absorbing life of a school which for him took on the character of the small but great good City where the minds and bodies of those within its privileged confines exceedingly flourished. The light which fell upon them to such effect came both from brilliant teaching and from the collective stimulus of vigorous youth in the charmed ambience of such a place at such a time.

In this atmosphere, and later in the equally potent forcing house of King's College, Cambridge, the intellectual, aesthetic and special talents of so gifted a young man as Keynes developed with every conceivable advantage on their side. His family exerted as positive an influence as did his educational environment. The length and character of his letters home from Eton provide evidence of this. Contrary to the more usual experience of boys' letters, those from Keynes became fuller and more detailed as he grew up through the school. The letters as an indication of the nature of Keynes's talents and the advantages he derived from Eton are well described by Sir Roy Harrod, his biographer.

> Every detail of school affairs was discussed: what work was being done—sometimes mathematical problems were transcribed in full—what games were played, what school events were taking place, how the other boys were progressing, the pros and cons of changes in curricula. The father got to know about Maynard's contemporaries so well that he could give a comprehensive forecast of their order in the Newcastle Prize examination.
> The letters show extremely clearly how absorbingly interested

Maynard was in the work, the games and the whole life of the school. It became his passion. It may certainly be claimed that Eton greatly helped his development. He found there associates who were congenial to him, youths of intellectual distinction with whom he could quickly get on to terms of intimacy on the basis of common interests. They had self-confidence, enquiring minds and a gay and carefree outlook. His own great fund of gaiety, of fun and satire, found scope. It is not clear that there are many schools in the world where one can find a wide choice of companions of this quality; it is clear that he needed this society and that in his schooldays his imagination was already stimulated and taking wing.

One Eton master only has left behind an adverse comment. He found the 16-year-old Keynes an irritating pupil. "He gives the idea of regarding himself as a privileged boy with perhaps a little intellectual conceit." Keynes wrote of his master "I could hardly have imagined that a man could be so dull . . . we have not yet succeeded in probing the depths of his ignorance."

Another master wrote of the young Keynes—"he certainly does command success to an amazing extent, but no one ever deserved it better."

Whole-hearted energy, tireless activity and enthusiasm, an unusually wide range of interests—these seem to be the most conspicuous qualities displayed by this unusual boy. He said himself at this time that a day of 36 hours and a week of 14 days would have suited him well. Naturally he seems to have taken the lead in everything that school life made possible—not only in academic work, but in games and in the wide-ranging interchange of ideas amongst those by nature fertile in such things. This he regarded at Eton, and continued to regard throughout his life, as certainly one of the main pleasures and perhaps one of the main objects of life. Because everything seemed to come easily to him, because he was immediately recognised as the natural spokesman in any group to which he belonged, because he was liked and respected by masters and boys, one would tend to think of Keynes at Eton as an out and out conformist. But this was not so on the evidence of his response to the outbreak of the Boer War. This produced a burst of officially inspired enthusiasm for the Volunteer Corps at Eton. Keynes wrote to his father asking whether he should join the throng of recruits and received a reply which pronounced no veto, but gave no encouragement. He took a day to make up his mind and then wrote home '. . . About the volunteers—I have not joined . . . I think that without your letter which amounted to a refusal I should have been compelled to be engulfed in this marvellous martial ardour that has seized the school. Some say that patriotism requires one to join the useless Eton shooters, but it seems to me to be the sort of patriotism that requires one to wave the Union Jack." The patriotism of Keynes was, right to the end of his life, of a more discriminating nature.

There were two other innate qualities which greatly developed in Keynes' school years. One was his capacity for friendship— the other his exceptional appetite for books. In spite of his tendency towards intellectual arrogance he possessed an unusually warm personality. Throughout his life pupils and colleagues, as well as those who had known him closely from school and college onwards, found in him an enormous source of support and pleasure. He was as reliable in friendship as he was stimulating and provocative. He was generous not only with money, but with time and effort. From his parents he derived a strong social conscience. He was convinced that the ablest members of society owed their duty and service to the rest. From the philosopher G. E. Moore and from his Cambridge friends, he took the gospel of the supreme claims of personal relationships—a gospel best expressed in the novels and essays of his friend, E. M. Forster.

Although specialising in mathematics, Keynes as a youth read voraciously in English literature and history. In 1900 for instance he was reading *The Ring and the Book* and twenty-two years later Roy Harrod records that he came into his Cambridge room to find him reading aloud *The Waste Land*. Furthermore he bought books all his life: in 1901 an 1820 edition of Wordsworth's *Excursion* from the subsequently famous bookstall in the market-place at Cambridge at the price of a shilling. His statistical interests prompted him to number the books he owned of substantial value or interest. By the time he entered King's College as an undergraduate the serial number had reached 329.

In almost all aspects what Keynes was later to become was immanent in the young man of 21. He was from the end of his first term one of "The Apostles"—that secret, high-minded, Cambridge society which had been described in *In Memoriam* by Tennyson, a former member.

He was President of the Union: he was soon to obtain his mathematical Honours; his second place in the open competition examination for the Civil Service, his fellowship of Kings, his job as a university teacher of economics. All these extraordinary successes presaged not, as so often, a life of comfortable progress up some conventional ladder to further success, but one of fierce struggle, conflict and disappointment. His was, above all, an existence marked by exceptional diversity of interests and activities. He was not only recognised as probably the most creative theoretical economist of his age but as a man of action. Much of his energy and genius was applied in the great critical debates which governed the world's political decisions after the first and second world wars. At the same time he was heavily engaged in journalism, literature and the patronage of the arts. He made a private fortune for himself and another for his college whose finances he handled for many years. He practised his talent for friendship and displayed his extraordinary gift for arousing affection and enthusiasm throughout his life. "As an economist," wrote Harrod, "he sought to bring about the well-being of mankind in the abstract; as a man he craved for the well-being of those with whom he had contact."

The education and early environment of H. G. Wells present the utmost contrast to those of J. M. Keynes. Wells, according to his superb *Experiment in Autobiography*,[2] published when he was 67, was born in 1866, blasphemous and protesting. His father was not a don but a gardener who had unwisely become the owner of a small, unprofitable crockery shop. As long as he remained fit, he was also able to earn something as a part-time cricket professional. Wells's mother, as he describes her, seems to come from the pages of Dickens. She was as god-fearing as she was incompetent—an innocent in a harsh world. The existance of the Wells family was perpetually threatened not only by financial disaster but by a general incapacity to cope. The flux of life brought this family, as so many others in that period, painful misfortune and repeated obstruction. All they sought was simple security, but the modest competence by which to achieve it always eluded them.

Keynes was born and brought up in 6 Harvey Road, Cambridge. Today this may seem a grim and comfortless house, but it must have been a palace compared with 47 High Street, Bromley where Wells spent the first thirteen years of his life. That was a dwelling dismal, insanitary, infested with bugs, but above all without hope and without prospects. For Keynes the world was wide open, for Wells it seemed hermetically sealed.

The objective of the small private school which the young Wells attended from the age of seven and a half to thirteen was the production of good clerks. This involved the ability to write English and to achieve accurate double entry book-keeping. Wells not only succeeded thus far, but made as much advance in mathematics as would a thirteen year old in a first class school today. It was a narrow but not a hopeless education. And now it seemed likely that it was all that Wells would receive, for he found himself, in response to his mother's ambition, apprenticed as a draper's assistant. Keynes for the next ten years of his life rode on the crest of a wave; Wells spluttered and struggled through not one but a succession of cruel, curling breakers. We have noted the qualities that underwrote Keynes's success, but how was it that Wells, with no initial advantage, was eventually to realise his potential to the full? The story has been fully told in his books. The Autobiography attributes what happened mainly to something which was shared with Keynes—an insatiable appetite for reading, developed at an early age and ravenous throughout his life.

"My leg was broken for me when I was between seven and eight," wrote Wells. "Probably I am alive today and writing this autobiography instead of being a worn-out, dismissed and already dead shop assistant because my leg was broken." Books were brought into his life as the direct result of this event—by his father from the Literary Institute and by the mother of the youth responsible for the accident. He read. As soon as he was fit again, father and mother endeavoured to discourage so unhealthy a habit, but to no avail.

Books came in again at the second decisive turn of events in the education of H. G. Wells. Mrs. Wells at last achieved an escape from the derelict shop at Bromley by returning to the employment of the ladies of Up Park, a Georgian mansion in West Sussex. There the young Wells, sacked after two months by the Windsor draper, was found a room and given the freedom of library, attics and park. The library provided an eighteenth century collection of bold and enlightening books, to use Wells' own description—Plato, Voltaire, *Gulliver's Travels*, *Rasselas* and Tom Paine are mentioned in the Autobiography. Inspired by such reading, by a mystical inner conviction of his own worth and by some teaching he managed to obtain from the able headmaster of the tiny local grammar school, Wells applied himself to the circumvention of each in turn of the maternal plans drawn up for his future. For him the life of the shop assistant brought with it the insufferable affront of loss of command over his own time. With an intelligence and an imagination restlessly active and perpetually hungry, Wells found niggling supervision unendurable. He was driven on by the desire to be himself, an ambitious, questing adolescent charged with the task of understanding the world around him and making something of his life. In place of self-determination, he was forced to comply with the dreary model of the conformist shop assistant. In revolt against the imposition of such a destiny, the young Wells was totally unscrupulous. He resorted eventually to the threat of suicide as a way to prise open his mother's grip. He refused humdrum servitude and engineered recognition of his intellectual cravings and an ingenious means of satisfying them.

Thus Wells made his fifth but not his final start in life as a kind of pupil teacher, a situation brilliantly described in his novel *Love and Mr. Lewisham*. At last his natural gifts for learning, that hungry appetite which no acute observer of his personality could possibly have missed, found satisfaction. By the time he was 18 Wells had won a place under T. H. Huxley at the new Normal School of Science in South Kensington. Immediately he faced challenges and demands new, but no less gruelling. His life was to be a battle-ground for another 61 years in which he was to publish more than 70 books and achieve a unique position in the world as one of the major prophets of a secular age.

Wells had his obvious weaknesses, but the gifts with which he was endowed enabled an extraordinary career to unfold. A sequence of obstacles and distractions beset his early years. It is hard to believe that more than one spirit in a million could have survived the repressive conditions of Wells's early life. To note the qualities in him which produced such astonishing success is to run over once again the signs by which an individual of high ability can be recognised. In Wells everything that one can think of was present. His energy, vitality, immense capacity for work and quickness of thought and action were perhaps the foremost of his gifts. It was his imagination which gushed-up the riches of his literary output and inspired the slow processing of his scientific, historical and philosophical thought. His vision and the originality of his mind can never be questioned. It was not the great, delicate, miraculously fashioned instrument that Keynes possessed. To hazard a guess Wells's I.Q. might have been 20 or 30 points below that of Keynes. The sub-title he gave to his autobiography was "Discoveries and Conclusions of a Very Ordinary Brain." Perhaps it wasn't so extraordinary a brain, but it *was* animated by an almost incredibly powerful and passionate spirit. The operations of the highly able depend not only on quotas of intelligence or degrees of creativity but on motivation and personality traits. The achievements of Wells exemplify this claim. It was his ambition, his divine discontent, his obstinacy, belligerency and self-confidence that counted most.

I take as a third case study of genius a contemporary of
H. G. Wells whose heredity was not dissimilar to that of Keynes,
but whose education and outlook differed vastly from both
Keynes's and Wells's. Rudyard Kipling's parents were gifted to
a marked degree. They must have been two of the most attractive
people of their time, but circumstances compelled them to the
peculiar act of abandoning their two children aged five and
three to the care of strangers whose name had been obtained
from an advertisement in the newspaper. Behind this decision
lay the fact that Lockwood Kipling earned his living in India
as an artist, teacher of art and museum curator. It was unthink-
able that young children should be brought up in India.
Rudyard had therefore to endure years of childhood misery
which left a permanent scar on his personality and of which he
recorded several vivid accounts.[3]

More than most of us Kipling inhabited a world of alternating
light and darkness. As a child this was true in a physical sense.
Soon after he had learned to read, and became dimly aware of
the bright possibilities that this skill could yield, he contracted
an eye trouble which at first cut off his new escape route altogether, and was to demand the wearing of high-powered lenses
throughout his life. It was true also in that the occasions when
he was free from his foster-parents and in the company of his
mother's gifted relations, and briefly (after five years) of his
mother herself, assumed by contrast with normal existence a
magically brilliant radiance. If ever the contentions of the
National Association of Gifted Children about the consequences
of neglecting the needs of such children was born out, it was in
the early life of Kipling. In his case a peculiar twisted, agonised,
even brutal outlook on human destiny clearly owed its origin
to these experiences. And yet out of misery and despair emerged
extraordinary achievement. What then were the talents of which
Kipling made such use?

An answer to this question can best be found in two of his
most famous books. They both take the form of autobiographical
fiction and were written when the events of his early life and his
educational experiences were easily recalled. *The Light that*

Failed opens with the early childhood years and goes on to describe meteoric successes as a young man and the outlook and style of life which resulted from them. *Stalky and Co* is a collection of incidents designed to convey a sense of what Kipling had derived from the school he attended between the ages of 11 and 16. They are both extraordinary, in many ways repellent, books, very different from the autobiographical novels of Wells —*Kipps, Mr. Lewisham* and *Tono-Bungay*—but equally gripping and widely read.

Kipling was at least as much affected by the suffering of his early life as was Keynes by his uninterrupted triumphs. It was not, to use his own words, "an unsuitable preparation for my future, in that it demanded constant wariness, the habit of observation and attendance on moods and tempers (of others); the noting of discrepancies between speech and action; a certain reserve of demeanour; and automatic suspicion of sudden favours."[4] His triumphs as a lucrative writer were owed to just these qualities. Kipling developed an altogether exceptional capacity to listen to the voices of other people, to observe their behaviour. His curiosity was unlimited; from all this data he fashioned imaginative extrapolation of compelling originality. His genius lay in his power of using words to fascinate, almost to hypnotise, his readers. No writer in the nineteenth or twentieth century struck so instant a vein of success. But the skills on which it depended had been deliberately cultivated by Kipling since his childhood. Essentially these skills were literary. Lack of that one skill or failure to develop it, would have left Kipling a very ordinary man.

It was certainly first, and probably always foremost, on books that he most depended. His outstanding power was that of absorbing the contents of written communication and, closely allied to it, no less a power of recall over the spoken word. His reading at school and before he went away to school was prodigious. Books inspired Wells to interpret life for himself and eventually to offer new interpretations of so compelling and original a nature that people all over the world looked to him as an intellectual leader. Kipling derived from his vast reading not a system of ideas, but a living current of incident and character. This he diverted to create his own stories and poems. His work is packed with literary allusion. Many of his plots are taken from actual happenings as recorded in army journals or Indian newspapers. Other are based on literary sources. The famous poem "If—" as Maurice Bowra discovered, seems to be a re-write of Browning's epilogue to *Asolando*. His plots are no more original than Shakespeare's.

The passion for reading was in part an outcome of intense innate curiosity, but it was greatly fostered by his unorthodox headmaster who gave the young Kipling the freedom of his magnificent personal library. Furthermore, he picked up the signs that indicated this particular boy's future achievement. He taught Kipling the discipline of writing and he revived the school magazine with Kipling as editor. Free from the demands of external examination, Kipling could steep himself in reading, writing and living with schoolboy energy and high appetite. Discipline was bred in him by experience. He learned to manage his own life and harness his own powers to work by the age of 15. At 16 he was back in India, regarding himself as engaged to a girl in England, and embarked on his career as a journalist. Kipling in fact was accepted for what he was, precociously mature, self-protective, single-minded and ablaze with a peculiar talent which he knew precisely how to use.

Keynes then provides an example of high ability early recognised and expensively nurtured; Wells of the struggle for recognition and then for conditions favourable to growth; Kipling of apparent neglect producing in the end singularly favourable conditions for the development of a single, all-embracing talent.

The creativity of these three men is only too clear. Yet their differences in personality are no less apparent—Keynes urbane, expansive, uninhibited; Wells hyper-active, insecure, irascible; Kipling acute, cautious, stoical. There is perhaps one common element to observe in the creative output of these diverse geniuses. They all reflected in their lives a daemonic impulse towards self-realisation, combined with a sense of mission towards all humanity. Both these characteristics are marks of the truly gifted.

CHAPTER VII

Able Boys and Able Girls

Some psychologists have resisted the suggestion that there are real differences in learning abilities between boys and girls. It is worth examining some of the relevant arguments, emerging from various types of research. But the educational attainment of boys and girls seems at present more influenced by family expectations and social morals than by hypotheses about mental ability. The virtual certainty that a girl is somewhat less likely to be a wanted child than a boy is one such influence. In education the fact that equal opportunities for girls is in this country of recent origin (if it can be said to exist at all) is obviously another. This is brought out if one chooses to compare the education received by Vera Brittain, the mother of the present Secretary of State for Education and that of Margaret Mead, the American anthropologist. Both were writers of autobiographies.

Vera Brittain was born in 1894 the daughter of the owner of paper mills in provincial England. What she learned up to the age of 11 came from her mother and a governess. Then she went to a school advertised as "for the daughters of gentlemen", and at 13 was sent away to a recently established girls' boarding school in the south of England. There the aspirations of the teachers and of the parents whose children attended the school were in conflict. Few parents had any desire that their daughters should be prepared for careers or even useful occupations. No entries for public examinations were made as a matter of normal routine. Nevertheless Vera Brittain profited from the one memorable teacher that so many pupils have found in schools of this kind. Under this lady's guidance and stimulus she read the newspapers or rather cuttings carefully selected from *The Times* and *The Observer*. She acquired some knowledge of world geography and she was inspired to read Shelley, Ruskin, Mrs. Humphrey Ward and Olive Schreiner. But the object of her education up to this point was essentially that of preparation for what she called "provincial young-ladyhood."

It was mere chance that decided her future otherwise. As a polite social occasion she attended Oxford University Extension lectures in Buxton Town Hall. After writing essays for the lecturer, the historian who later became Sir John Marriott, she was accepted for the Oxford Extension Summer School and eventually, largely self-taught, succeeded in obtaining a minor scholarship at Somerville College. "But so unpopular," she records, "at that time (1914) was the blue stocking tradition, and so fathomless the depth of provincial self-satisfaction, that my decision to go to an English town to study the literature of my own language caused me to be labelled 'ridiculous' and 'eccentric'. How *can* you send your daughter to college?" said a neighbour to her mother. "Don't you ever want her to get married?"[1]

Margaret Mead by contrast was the child of an American University professor and of a very remarkable mother, an impassioned feminist, deeply serious and highly educated. The surprising thing is that with such a background, school and later college occupied relatively uninspiring stretches of her life. Her parents chose to live in a different place each year. Each place was regarded by her mother not only in terms of what schools it offered, but of what local talent was available, artistic, constructional, athletic, religious or agricultural, to give an additional fillip to her children's education. From six onwards Margaret Mead generally went to a school of some kind for at least half the day. All the succeeding years provided her, she records, with "informal education and occasional hit-or-miss, inappropriate schooling which served to educate me in American culture but did little to prepare me for formal academic work."[2]

Reading and writing (stories, poems and plays) became her greatest early pleasures. What she called "the continuous running commentary" of her extended family was clearly the supreme educative influence in her childhood. What she listened to was discussion of the society into which she was growing up, radical views on its strengths and weaknesses, hopeful aspirations for its future, which were held greatly to depend on the quality of the State's educational provision. Margaret Mead, unlike other children, never heard taxes mentioned, she tells us, except in terms of their being too low. All her life she had expected to go to college and this she did, not after a struggle, such as Vera Brittain's, but naturally and easily at the age of 17.

Here then were two girls, living at much the same time, not dissimilar in ability, but children of two totally different cultures—in no respect more different than in that of attitudes to education. The received opinion of the middle class in provincial England distinguished firmly between what was due in this matter to boys and what was due to girls. In America no such distinction was made. Margaret Mead set off for California to attend her father's old college because a temporary set-back to the family's material fortunes made her mother's old college in the East a rather too expensive proposition. How her dissatisfaction with this mixed college compared with Vera Brittain's strong feelings of respect for Somerville must be discussed later when we come to differences between gifted young women and gifted young men.

Physical sex differences arise from the presence in men of certain chromosomes and their absence in women. In accordance with this distribution, the pattern of nerve cells in the brain develops somewhat differently in the male child. Eventually these differences lead to a second phase of sex development and the production of male and female hormones. Until puberty the muscular strength of boys and girls will not greatly differ, but by the age of 16 boys are of course considerably bigger and stronger.

What is happening all this time to the growth and development of intellectual and imaginative faculties?

Generalized surveys show very little difference between the performance of boys and girls in formal tests of intelligence, at any rate in their earlier years. There is, however, a substantial body of test evidence to support the view that little girls are better at verbal skills and boys at such special, visual skills as those required by jig-saw puzzles. This is normally explained by the biologists as the result of differences between the brain development of boys and girls. Some psychologists on the other hand believe that there is evidence to suggest that the differences between these abilities in boys and girls may be due rather to the earlier physical maturation of girls. Late developing children are generally boys, but whatever their sex, they appear to have superior visuo-spatial ability compared with those who reach puberty early.

Skills in reading have been studied over a long period in this country. It is believed that on the whole girls make faster initial progress in learning to read and in acquiring powers of speech. Towards the age of 10, however, boys in Burt's opinion are tending to outstrip girls and his contention (dating from 1923) seems to be borne out by the national standards of Reading Surveys carried out in 1948, 1952 and 1956. The survey conclusions may be misleading because the main test used (Watts/Vernon) contained material of greater interest to boys. It was noted from the results of the first survey that "very good readers among girls are as good as boys, average ones are a little poorer and very poor readers are less frequent."[3] This was confirmed by the 1956 results in the case of eleven- and fifteen-year-olds. Only in the rural schools was the mean score for girls of eleven superior to that of boys. In all types of school and area, boys had the advantage at that age, and by the age of fifteen their lead had been slightly increased.

The tests carried out in 1970/71 by the National Foundation for Educational Research[4] confirmed the supposition that the girls were never so good as the boys at one extreme, nor as bad as them at the other. But it produced a somewhat surprising result from the fifteen-year-olds where, even on the Watts/ Vernon test, girls now did better than boys. The other test used (NS6) was of more recent origin and had shown no consistent bias in favour of either sex. The mean scores attained on this test showed a somewhat greater superiority on the girls' part. Our chief interest, however, is in the top 10%. There boys showed slightly to better advantage at 11 in both tests. At fifteen girls had certainly caught up, but not acquired any significant lead.

The question that demands an answer when one considers the education of the most able girls, such as Margaret Mead and Vera Brittain, is whether they tend to be gifted in any particular sex-limited direction. Do they possess talents distinctively different from those shown by able boys? Should they be treated alike or are there types of special attention desirable for one sex and not of any great importance to the other?

It cannot be said that those questions have been at all fully investigated. If any generalisations are ventured they must be treated with reserve. There are obviously social and cultural factors, regional variations and aspects of the educational system itself that will need to be examined and taken into account. There can be little doubt for instance that from an early age the interests of boys and girls separate themselves. Is this because girls *choose* dolls and boys guns, or because dolls and guns are pushed in front of them? Do little girls *actually* inherit a maternal instinct and little boys a hunting/fighting instinct or is it merely that our own culture assumes this to be the case? We do not know.

It would be mistaken, however, to abandon our interest in these questions, especially now when political efforts are being made to redress a balance of opportunity, heavily weighted against women. In matters of educational planning it might be thought that attention to the special needs of girls has decreased rather than been intensified in recent years. This would surely be a pity. Differences between talented boys and talented girls do reveal themselves. There is no reason to believe that they need affect the accepted practice of differentiating little, if at all, between the programmes adopted for boys and girls in the primary school; but there are probably useful things to be done at this early stage so that the school may counteract some of the influences that adversely affect the later education of able girls. What might these things be?

A glance at the past can be helpful. When the Consultative Committee under Hadow's chairmanship considered the state of primary education it took evidence from teacher witnesses on supposed emotional and intellectual differences between the sexes. It summed-up this evidence as follows:

> Girls at this age frequently exhibited greater facility of expression in writing; they were capable of rather more sustained effort and often produced more painstaking work than boys. They excelled in patient and persevering attention to details, in jumping by rapid processes of intuition to presumptive conclusions. Boys, on the other hand, were inclined to be more plodding and methodical in their processes of thought, and perhaps more critical of their own conclusions; they were less diffuse and less verbose. They appeared to be more alive to the exact content of phrases and forms of statement. Many witnesses had observed that girls showed a keen desire for neatness and beauty in their work. Both boys and girls were unable at this stage of development to concentrate for long periods on set tasks, though they might concentrate on some voluntary effort. Both sexes, for some years from about the age of ten, seemed to desire to express themselves through drawing, handicraft, and other practical activities, rather than through speech. Boys, however, often appeared to be readier than girls to work with their hands, and displayed more interest in mechanical matters. In general, boys were described by several witnesses as being more unconventional and irresponsible than girls at this stage, though other teachers had observed that boys seems to have more respect for rules and regulations than girls. Girls were said to be more ready to pass moral judgement, usually of blame, than boys.[5]

Primary Education, the 1959 volume of suggestions, prepared by H.M. Inspectors for the use of teachers, makes little distinction between the teaching of boys and the teaching of girls. It remarks that "*most* boys and *some* girls (my italics) want to see how things work, and primary education as a whole has not yet taken full advantage of this youthful curiosity about mechanical and technical things." *Post hoc, propter hoc*—considering that three quarters of the primary teachers were women it is surprising that the causal connection between the first and second parts of of the sentence was not pointed out.

Differences between girls and boys which seem to become apparent at some point in the junior school are commented on in general terms.

"They move and behave differently, and their interests sometimes divide them; they differ in their choice of stories and of books, in the subjects of their writing and in what they collect. The girls may be maturing physically more quickly than the boys, while the boys may perhaps show more daring and enterprise."[6]

But when considering in detail the various components of the primary school curriculum, the book has virtually nothing to say about sex discrimination. Even the obviously different interests and aptitudes in physical education are played down. The question of whether hobbies and interests are the result of sex differences, or of the attitudes of parents and teachers, is left open. A long chapter headed Art, Craft and Needlework deplores the recommendation of the Cross Commission in 1888 that boys should do "linear drawing" as an alternative to the "plain sewing" for girls. Conceding that there are differences of interest in the later years of the junior school, it is pointed out that "many girls continue to enjoy handling clay, cardboard and sometimes wood, and boys still turn to fabrics, needle and thread as they need them." Girls, it is wisely observed, want just as much as boys to enjoy the pleasure of discovering how things are made, and to see an ambitious construction carried through to its conclusion.

The Plowden Report is even more reserved and indeed enigmatic on these matters. As an example one might look at two things in which the parents of primary school children are keenly interested—their emotional development and the

question of discipline. On the first of these the report has several
excellent pages, but they contain no indication that children are
of more than one sex. Then comes the one brief passage that
recognises this fact and yet reads as inconsequentially as a child's
essay.

> Even at the ages with which we are concerned, boys and girls
> develop at different rates and react in different ways—a fact
> which needs particular attention because we have co-educational
> schools. Boys are more vulnerable to adverse environmental
> circumstances than girls. Both reach maturity earlier than they
> did.[7]

It is never made clear what kind of attention is indicated
although much later in the report it is stated that girls have the
knack of gaining the approval of their teachers and are thus
unfairly favoured when a system of streaming is employed.

On discipline there is a curious sentence suggesting that it
is boys rather than girls who need "to feel the pressure of
authority in order to come to terms with it." Nevertheless the
report with one dissenting voice (a woman's) recommended the
discontinuance of corporal punishment for boys and girls
alike.

If the main volume of the Plowden Report seems unhelpful,
this is not the case with the volume of research reports which
contains the invaluable National Child Development Study of
children born in 1958. One thing this showed was that both in
tests of "problem arithmetic", and in teachers' rating of number
work, the ablest seven-year-olds were found significantly more
frequently amongst boys than girls. In oral ability girls were
rated above boys but in general knowledge their rating was
reversed. When a sample of the most gifted of these children
was again studied[8] at the age of 11 the same proportion of girls
and boys proved above average in mathematics, but more boys
appeared in the very top group. More boys had also reached the
highest level of oral ability. An important table is included,
showing in respect of what particular abilities teachers had
nominated the children they judged to be of "outstanding

ability". Very marked superiority was accorded to girls in English, writing stories, and music. Boys were much more frequently nominated as outstanding in mathematics, science and craft work and a little more frequently in art.

The superior verbal, reading and all-round language ability of eleven-year-old girls was also recorded by the battery of tests administered in connection with the Barker Lunn study of the effects of streaming in primary school.[9] These tests were again used to establish a high ability group from amongst the children whose progress in French at their primary schools was studied by Clare Burstall.[10] The children so selected (about 13% of the total whose response to French was studied) could thus be regarded as having the highest potential for language learning. When tests of proficiency in oral French were given, there was a marked tendency in the sample as a whole for girls to score higher than boys. Among those who showed high ability in the French tests (one standard deviation above the mean calculated for their school group) two-thirds were girls.

We now have some picture of what appear to be certain distinctions between the nature of boys' and girls' ability in their earlier years. In a society in which the education of boys, beyond an elementary stage, has a much longer tradition than that of girls, it is certainly worth considering whether the present arrangements for secondary and further education take into account the handicap from which girls are bound to suffer. If it is true that girls have an innate difficulty in acquiring visuo-spatial skills, due to the sex chromosomes, then should there not be special steps taken to correct it? More of their early years at school might be spent with three dimensional objects and apparatus which stimulate understanding of spatial relation-ships, and less on mechanical arithmetic. If it is true that girls acquire reading skills earlier than boys, then this should be recognised by giving them more advanced books to read instead of allowing them to consume more and more "readers", graded to the level which they have already passed. If general knowledge of the world and its history is known to be a weak-ness of girls, primary teachers ought to make special efforts to correct it. Programmes of work in history, geography and science ought to be re-examined with the aim of making them more attractive to girls.

This book's purpose is to draw attention to the danger and injustice of neglecting the educational needs of the most able children we have. At the age of eleven at least half these children are girls. It is my contention that able girls are particular sufferers from the present weaknesses in English education at the primary stage. Certainly girls are disproportionately affected by the national attitudes to secondary education and the current patterns of teaching and organisation that have evolved. 50% of the ablest eleven-year-olds are girls, but the proportion of girls applying recently to English and Welsh Universities was only 34·5% in 1975 and had risen to 35·4% in 1976. Of those who are now completing their studies in pure science, engineering and technology about 19,000 are men and over just 4,000 are women.

One conclusion is inescapable. Many able pupils disappoint expectation during their years at a secondary school. There is a strong probability that a great many more of these children are girls than boys. It might then be argued that the clever girl lacks qualities of persistence that are to be found in the clever boy. Or one could conclude that secondary schooling as at present organised favours boys. Alternatively the explanation may be found outside the educational system altogether.

A searching study[11] of bright under-achievers carried out in England, America and Australia by one particularly well qualified to observe and draw conclusions shows the severe handicaps imposed on secondary school pupils and particularly girls by family demands. These bear most heavily on the intelligent eldest child in a family placed in the lowest socio-economic class.

The whole climate of our society is one in which boys are stimulated to pursue courses that may provide them with qualifications and career prospects of many kinds. Girls on the other hand are assumed to aspire to an early marriage and to aim at earnings based on short intensive training, rather than on longer, continuous processes of education. We are not yet emancipated from a nineteenth century social philosophy which set educational institutions the task of training girls in useful skills and gracious leisure-time pursuits. "Provincial young ladyhood" is an out-of-date phrase but an enduring aspiration. Its realisation may now include entry into the job market as a secretary, a model, or a receptionist, but it still remains an influential concept. Many parents and many able girls want nothing more than the style and degree of education appropriate to these ends.

Another point that seems to emerge fairly clearly from the observation of secondary school teachers is that able boys tend to be more single-minded in cultivating their talents. They form more positive ideas of their career prospects and the steps necessary to realise their ambitions. A good deal of sound experience lay behind a section of the Crowther Report[12] which was subsequently much criticised. This asserted that "single-mindedness" was "the spring from which the disinterested pursuit of knowledge swells" . . . Specialisation and "subject-mindedness" were regarded as the main emotional impetus towards intellectual effort. Such views were of course derived largely from experience in boys' grammar schools and independent schools for boys. It was related to that 6% of the school population—the most able boys and girls—who intended to enter a university. In the 1950s this group was overwhelmingly composed of boys. In the sixth forms of independent schools, recognised as efficient, they were four times as numerous, according to figures given in the Crowther Report. Even more startling figures are found in the Second Report of the Public Schools Commission[13]. These show university entrants in the year 1967-8 and are percentages of the school leavers in that year.

Direct Grant		Maintained Secondary (including Grammar)		Independent recognised as efficient	
Boys	Girls	B	G	B	G
47.9	29.1	6.1	3.1	30.3	11.4

These figures seem to supply convincing evidence of the wasted talents of many of the most able girls in English secondary schools. We shall have to consider whether a system reorganised into comprehensive schools and sixth form colleges may not already show indications of improving the position. But first there is the question of the subject choices of clever boys and girls to be considered. It is reasonable to assume that these young people will aim at obtaining good A-level results. It would also be fair to say that their school will be doing all in its power to help them further their ambitions. Examination success is likely to be more highly valued than idealistic concepts of a balanced general education by both school and pupil. The most able pupils are also going to be those who pursue well-established academic subjects and not the more varied and diffused and quasi-vocational studies which now tend to be provided for the less able. The choice of subjects at A-level is bound to be governed by O-level choices and results. These in their turn will to some extent depend on what subject choices a particular school is able to offer and that depends on the options taken up often in the second or third year of the pupil's secondary education. In the fourth and fifth years the common curriculum normally comprises religious education, English, mathematics and physical education for all pupils, to which groups of optional studies are added according to what the particular school can offer. It is here that the differences in the opportunities open to girls and boys occur, as is shown in figures derived from a recent survey by H.M. Inspectors.[14] They show, for instance, that art was offered to almost the whole school population, but physics was available much more readily to boys than to girls and biology and music somewhat more readily to girls than to boys. In the popularity of subjects striking differences occur.

Options in the fourth and fifth forms

(Percentages of pupils being offered and taking particular subjects)

| | | Being offered | Taking |
		Per cent of total	Per cent of total
Physics	Boys	90	47
	Girls	71	12
Chemistry	Boys	79	27
	Girls	76	17
Biology	Boys	88	28
	Girls	95	49
French	Boys	84	24
	Girls	89	40
German	Boys	36	5
	Girls	40	8
Geography	Boys	67	37
	Girls	63	29
History	Boys	67	29
	Girls	62	29
Art	Boys	97	37
	Girls	98	36
Music	Boys	73	9
	Girls	85	13

These figures are introduced to emphasise the extent to which the subjects chosen by clever girls for their school leaving examination at 18 are pre-determined. The percentages of those actually taking A-level courses is shown on facing page:

Subject	All Boys	All Girls
Mathematics	41	15
Further pure mathematics	9	3
Physics	41	9
Chemistry	30	13
Biology	16	21
English literature	23	53
French	8	24
German	3	9
Geography	27	22
History	23	28
Economics	22	8
Art	9	15
Music	2	4

Between three and four times as many clever boys take mathematics and sciences (biology excluded) while three times as many clever girls take modern languages. It is little comfort to know that the same or an even worse position obtains in the High Schools of the U.S.A. One of the reasons is quite clearly to be found in the trend towards co-education. A much higher proportion of girls in single-sex schools took mathematics, physics and chemistry than in mixed schools. Twice as many boys in single-sex schools took French as in mixed schools.

At this point, the reflections of the seventeen-year-old Margaret Mead in her first weeks at college are worth considering. "As long as I was in High School the greater maturity of adolescent girls had not struck me. But in the setting of this co-educational college it became perfectly clear both that bright girls could be better than bright boys and that they would suffer for it. This made me feel that co-education was thoroughly unattractive. I neither wanted to do bad work in order to make myself attractive to boys nor did I want them to dislike me for doing good work. It seemed to me that it would be much simpler to go to a girl's college where one could work as hard as one pleased."

To this personal view one might add the statement of a parent, as reported by Miss Hitchfield, and the opinion of a very experienced teacher of able girls, Mrs. Warnock. The parent, asked what type of secondary school she would have wanted for her able daughter, answered, "We would have chosen a grammar school—a greater percentage go to university. It's essential at school to mix with children who want to go to university. The parent has to keep reminding the child that they want to do something better when they're mixing with children who all they want to do is to get out and earn money. For different children—different things. It's important for her to find out the subject she really excels in— and keep at that."

The conscientiousness of able girls is emphasised by Mrs. Warnock who pleads that they should be given the chance to develop one genuine enthusiasm to an advanced level. "In my experience intelligent people being educated at school in the way that for the time being we think it proper that they should, namely working towards three 'A' levels, feel passionately that they have not enough time to think about their subjects. They cannot, they feel, do them properly at all.. .."[15]

Enough has been said at the least to suggest that there are differences between the types of ability possessed by able boys and those displayed by girls of equal intellectual power. Even if this is unproved, there are factors arising from custom and convention in our society, and from its social institutions, which influence girls to move in one direction and boys in another. Boys do tend to reveal different attitudes to academic work, different styles of learning and a different range of subject interests. Responses to methods of teaching and to the kinds of relationships developed between teacher and pupil are also likely to differ. Generalisation to the effect that more clever boys will be convergent thinkers and more girls divergent thinkers are probably unjustified. There is no reason to infer, from the fact that many more able girls study literature and music, that they are all more creative or more imaginative than the able boys whose preference is for chemistry and economics.

The one profoundly disturbing aspect of the questions raised in this chapter is the apparent conspiracy of silence about them.

In the mass of documents, reports, investigations and enquiries which have dealt with English education in recent years almost nothing of significance has been written about learning differences and types of ability in boys and girls of secondary school age. This is true of the whole ability range. In the case of the most able the neglect of these matters is particularly marked and particularly serious.

There occurred a sadly neglected opportunity when the Public Schools Commission reported in 1970 on the direct grant, grant-aided and independent day schools. About 5% of the school population were then educated in them, but of course a much higher proportion of those doing advanced work. There were roughly equal numbers of girls and boys. The report concluded with a chapter called "Educating the most Gifted" in which majority and minority proposals were advanced. The views on both sides, expressed by these distinguished Commissioners, were somewhat stereotyped and highly predictable. There was a bland assumption that what is good for boys must be equally good for girls. Much concern was expressed by the majority about social divisions which should not be tolerated. "The society we hope this country will become" is mentioned but its character is not specified. The minority argued that the most able "need competition from other pupils with like ability," and that "able pupils and teachers must both be concentrated in schools of a special kind."

Indifference to the evidence that conditions and procedures for educating able boys may be ill-suited to the needs of able girls was characteristic of both parties. The Commission contained historians who cannot have reflected on the historic struggle to obtain any kind of academic education for girls in this country. It sadly lacked an anthropologist like Margaret Mead to force on its attention the educational inequalities which arise within a culture still dominated by male values.

CHAPTER VIII

Adults and the Able Child

Relationships with adults are of course vital to the development of all children and they begin at birth. Mother and child are bound together by functional ties which are extremely powerful and indeed central to the well-being of both. It is, however, within the mother's power to objectify this relationship, that is to say, she can, if she so wishes, step outside the situation, in which she has been allotted the protective role, and look in on the inter-play of her own and her child's personalities. Thus she can observe the demands each makes on the other. She may conclude, when she has achieved this detachment, that in some particular way what she is doing for her child may be ill-judged or that certain habits which the child is developing may be harmful to its future.

Two trivial examples can illustrate the point. The young child screams when it is given its bath simply because the mother has not the experience to know that the water is too hot for his sensitive skin. She decides in future to test the temperature with her elbow instead of with her fingers and hand. All is well, but the problem which appears to arise in the second instance is more complex. The mother notices that her baby is forming the habit of sucking his thumb. Her mind goes to work on this observation. Is it harmful? Should it be prevented? The answers are almost certainly no to both questions. But why does it happen and should she do anything at all about it?

These are much more fruitful questions to ask, but it is not easy to answer them. The remote possibility that the shape of the child's mouth may ultimately be affected by the habit is relatively unimportant. The immediate possibility that the habit may be a symptom of something disturbing here and now in the life of the child deserves rather more of the mother's attention. One may assume that the child derives from the thumb sucking some positive relief or pleasure. If there should be a strong desire (perhaps on aesthetic grounds) for this to be replaced by some equal but alternative satisfaction, then such must be provided. Such an alternative may be found in a change of feeding or sleeping arrangements. It is possible that more talking and playing, more companionship and demonstrative affection has to be found.

Thus the mother's connection with her child is generally on the plane of action. The child undoubtedly learns from her, but he learns because of what she does, not because of what she says. The manner of the child's learning is reciprocal at this early stage and wholly dependent on what goes on between himself and the caring adult. But this reciprocity, the playing off of one person against another, is not the inter-action of two equals. The mother and her child do appear to possess a peculiarly sensitive understanding of each other's behaviour. It is not difficult to distinguish an entirely different note and purpose in a baby's crying when it is with its mother and the same baby's cry when directed towards relative strangers. The infant cries for its mother's ears in the expectation that something will be done in response to its cry. But that is by no means the only possible explanation. The baby may cry simply because it is angry or because it is sad. These are two distinct kinds of crying easy enough to recognise apart. Exasperating though it may be, an outburst of noisy rage indicates that the child is acquiring experience of human life, and is learning how to cope with it. An angry baby seems to be at odds not merely with a single source of pain, which could be removed, but with the whole human predicament. He cries in this fashion because he believes that in some general way things could be better, and that if there is to be any improvement, it will depend on the action of the mother or of some other adult. The child rages against a world in which this action, so necessary, so obvious, as he understands the situation, is not being taken. Rage is an act of faith; it expresses a belief that something could be done, that change might be change for the better. So far from being an expression of hate, the angry crying of a child is a recognition that love exists in the world. The child who has no experience of love, no faith and no belief will also cry, but in a despairing, disillusioned way and in the end perhaps will resort to some meaningless self-destructive gesture, such as banging his head against a wall.[1] An able child whose education has been neglected in this particular way may eventually react to life in a similar manner.

Adult and child are unequal because the adult is further on the way to becoming a complete person than is the child. Completeness lies in finding out how to understand oneself, as the Delphic Oracle pointed out. It is necessary to reconcile the orderly, rational conscious self with the chaotic, uncontrolled, unconscious elements of personality. There is on the one hand passive contentment and the security of self-love, on the other, active response to the various forms of challenge which life presents, above all, perhaps, our dangerous propensity to love others. Destiny compels us to give as well as to take and to give means to risk rejection. Acceptance or apparent rejection by the adult world will be one of the principal determining factors in the education of the most able.

Parents know perfectly well that a baby's survival depends on their physical intervention on its behalf. But their baby's wants and needs, which were at first few and simple, develop with extraordinary speed; they become bewilderingly diverse and difficult to define. The first lessons—learning to breathe and learning to suck—are soon mastered. Thereafter the child is embarked on a course of study in which there are no quick or easy answers. All that goes up to make human life has, step by step, to be investigated. What am I? What can I do? What has life to offer? Very soon it appears that a child has to wrestle with baffling questions of this kind. The father's physical strength, the mother's loving protective instincts serve so well to provide for a young child's earliest needs. But as these new directions open up what similar resources can be assembled?

Most parents and children have help poured on them from all sides. To invite adult interest in their child, within the extended family and beyond, is among the natural instincts of young parents. People are from the beginning, therefore, concerned and affected. Countless playthings are procurable: objects of interest and satisfaction to the child exist everywhere. In response to people and things, learning is initiated and the particular leanings of the individual are often indicated. High levels of intelligence and imaginative vigour can be observed in young children and can be seen to develop in the same way as do their physical powers. The help given by adults towards the growth and development of all these qualities is likely to be most effective when imbued with an understanding of the way children learn. Experience with the very young provides insight into the general conditions that promote learning. It is obvious, for instance, that some kind of unique inter-personal connection exists between mother and baby. The earliest, the most intense and far-reaching of bonds is that between the mother and the child at the breast. Psychologists believe that in the tensions aroused, the excitement released and the satisfaction obtained, this relationship can only be compared to that between mature individuals in acts of physical love.

In all situations where the young are learning from their elders, some connection of this kind has to exist. Teaching is not a mechanical process but an expression of feeling towards another individual. Unless two individuals give, and take from each other, some real element, nothing that can be called education will occur. Adult and child must be bonded together in such a way that a flow of help from one to the other is released. This process should bring happiness to them both.

Something else is equally important as a foundation on which learning can be built. A child can only learn effectively from an adult who is himself capable of learning. The adult must be

H

consciously concerned with his own, or her own, search for
maturity and completeness. All must be aware of the discipline of
reconciliation, of the controls on appetites and aggressions
which are demanded. Courage and faith are qualities which,
shown in children, give intense satisfaction to adults. We feel,
when they demonstrate these qualities, that our children are on
their way to achieving a hold on life. Everything they do to
express joy and confidence fills us with pleasure. We need to be
satisfied that the existence we have imposed on them has
released within their being those vital currents of volition without which (so our experience has told us) life cannot be properly
lived. It follows that to teach children to be brave, happy and
trusting, adults must themselves cultivate these qualities. And
for only a few of us are they easily acquired, but without them
this search for personal unity, wholeness, self-responsibility
cannot be advanced.

It is worth noting that in Tolstoy's novel *Anna Karenina*
Levin's reconciliation with life, the fact that "it is no longer
meaningless as it was before, but has a positive meaning of
goodness with which I have the power to invest it" comes to
him as a result of two experiments owed to the children in his
house. First, when his wife and baby are sheltering from a
thunderstorm in a wood nearby, one of the trees is seen to be
struck by lightning. Levin rushes out to discover that they are
safe in another part of the wood. That night Levin sees how his
little son responds for the first time with a happy smile as his
parents squeeze a sponge over his naked body. And previously
he has been struck by the "passive, weary scepticism" with which
the older children receive their mother's remonstrances after
they have discovered for themselves the joys of making raspberry
jam in cups held over lighted candles and "squirting milk into
each others' mouth like fountains." The children don't need to
worry about whether cups will be broken or milk wasted. They
want to invent something new of their own and not to care about
its practical results. One must live for completeness, Levin
concludes, for the achievement of some standard not set by
reason, but by life itself when suffused with faith and imagination.

It is not easy for parents and teachers obsessed with their caring responsibilities to grasp that what they are is more important in the long run than what they do. Yet this is what experience seems to suggest. It is possible to care with too much zeal, to watch over a child in altogether too exclusively protective a spirit. The anxieties reflected by unremitting attention to shielding the child from remotely possible danger may themselves produce tension and insecurity in the live object of all that care and affection. Of course it is necessary to watch over small children, but equally important that they should enjoy relaxed conditions and a tranquil, rather than a nervous, environment. Caring demands that one should refuse to become obsessed by danger. Teaching depends more on possessing an awareness of what the child *can* do, than on worrying about the failures and mistakes. All adults should cherish the moments of reward and excitement of which they become acutely aware when they perceive certain marks of humanity start up within their children. The qualities on which civilisation depends—zest, affection, ingenuity, persistence, consideration for others—can all be seen in young children. The mother hears her baby's first living cry: Levin watches the rejoicing smile so closely following on a moment of intense anxiety: the teacher notes the effect of the creative enterprise of a single child on the co-operative effort in some creative enterprise of a whole pupil group. Such events can only be responded to by joy, however anxious or oppressed the life of the adult may be. We should never miss the dramatic quality of our existence among children with its lightning changes from happy excitement to minor tragedy, from achievement to frustration, from laughter to tears.

Nevertheless adults are bound to believe that there are positive things they must do. There are occasions when they must remonstrate. The child has his wishes which the adult may not feel called upon to satisfy, but he must pay attention to them. The adult has his wishes too, and to make certain demands on the child is human behaviour which the child will respect, even if he does put up an opposition. In the case of the very young the adult wants the child to be clean, co-operative, controlled and reasonably obedient as much as he wants an immediate happiness to shine out. The child wants the adult to be always present, always powerful enough to provide for his needs, and for adult failure the child wants an explanation. Explanations are the very central core of the adult's part in children's learning. The child's wants are instinctive and often irrational, but much of what the adult wants is carefully considered, reflecting standards and beliefs held as a result of education and experience. The parents and the teacher have in mind appropriate and effective ways of inducing children to accept these standards and adopt these beliefs. How then must they proceed?

There are really only two alternatives open to the adults at this point. In all education in which they are involved their tendency must be towards one or the other—the one is composed of all that cluster of ideas and behaviours that centres round the word "communication" and the other has its primary symbol in the word "training". We must take a closer look at where the difference lies. Training comes first because the meanings associated with the word are relatively simple; it is not a word to be despised. There are many situations where we would rather be a trained man than a raw recruit. Most of us have reason to be thankful to those who trained us in some specific aspect of life or work. But training has its limitations. One can be trained to kill efficiently but not to die with dignity. Training may be the right word for a mother's influence on a child's control over its bowels and bladder. It is not the word we would use for what influence parents may exert on the way the genital organs of their children are used throughout their lives.

It seems a platitude to say that teaching takes place best by means of communication, but this is only when we use the word in the sense of transmitting a message. It also means exchanging messages, a two-way process, and more subtly it can mean entering into communion, of which the essence is the mutuality of the relationships. There may be an element of training in the education of children but even those who insist most vehemently on this aspect of the process have to recognise the significance of other elements. Training may be (and sometimes is) given by impersonal teaching machines. Education implies a human relationship in which the mind and the feelings of teacher and pupil are involved. If the essence of education is the passing of messages between adult and child, then the form of the message, and the mechanisms by which it is transmitted and received are all-important. Effective education takes place only when answers are found to these problems.

If then we are to regard the creation of the proper adult-child or teacher-pupil relationship as the foundation on which education rests, what are the particular difficulties of achieving this in the case of gifted children? How does the parent divide attention and support between one member of his family whose demands arise from an unusually active mind and another who lacks mental initiative? What should a teacher do to meet the special needs of a very able child in a class of merely average ability?

Parents of course can, and do, make very serious mistakes. We have already noted how mistaken was Mrs. Joseph Wells in her expectations of her son and how misplaced were her interventions in what she saw as his best interests. And the admirable and highly intelligent parents of Rudyard Kipling condemned him to early childhood years which so outraged his feelings that the mark they made on him endured throughout his life. But on the whole gifted children are particularly prized by their parents. It is more likely that they will receive too much, rather than too little, attention. It is true that parental ambition may hinder them, and that their particular qualities can so totally conflict with the normal expectations of parents, themselves of below average ability, that a break-down of communication can occur. Parents often do need and often seek help and support from others in bringing up their very able children. But no one supposes that such help is necessary on the scale, or at the cost, of that required in the case of those severely handicapped, either mentally or physically. As Mr. Tom Hart has pointed out, writing about problem children who truant from school, "If you've an I.Q. of 130, you're missed in a week. If it's 66 it takes them 18 months to notice you've gone."[2]

Miss Hitchfield was convinced by the research she did that the parents of gifted children show greater concern and interest in their children's education than parents in general. She found no reason to think that special difficulties occur in the relationships between gifted children and their parents, except in a small number of cases. The problem, as she sees it, occurs when family conditions or absence of resources impose constrictions on the strivings of the gifted child for knowledge and skills. Parental neglect in such cases is less due to absence of concern than to ignorance, impatience or outside pressures.

The teacher will of course be coping with a larger group of children than the parent. In the nature of things the ability range will be wider, but the teacher's aim will normally be to provide help to every child with whom she is concerned and of a kind suited to its individual capacity. Complete success in so demanding a task is seldom possible. It is most likely to occur where the channels of communication are most open; and this, it has been argued here, is something dependent on the right inter-personal relationships. Such relationships can only grow as the teacher obtains knowledge of the child and the child knowledge of the teacher. Thus the teacher must first secure and hold the attention of her pupil; she must register herself in his mind as a personality reflecting certain principles, values and predictable patterns of behaviour. To obtain knowledge of the children some regard must be paid to records maintained by other teachers, and perhaps some testing of ability and attainment may be helpful. There should certainly be discussion with parents. But principally it is her own power to observe and assess that a good teacher employs.

Once it is clear that certain children not merely possess more existential skill but are capable of working at a faster pace and with deeper penetration than the rest, then a conscientious teacher will take certain steps on their behalf. She will already be preparing work at different levels for children of varying ability and may find that the amount of preparation necessary to provide for the very able is extremely demanding. There are other adults in the school, including the Head, whose help might be enlisted. The material resources at the disposal of the class may have to be increased to meet the special need that has arisen —books and apparatus of a more advanced kind than the particular class has previously used, for instance. Assignments and targets set will have to be of a challenging nature. There should be no mistaking the boredom and frustration of gifted children if the pace or interest of the work set them is insufficient.

Practical measures of this kind will come easily to the skilled and experienced teacher, but they may present an insecure beginner with intractable problems. The situation of a particular child with marked ability will be that much worse if the teacher concerned adopts the not unfashionable view that a class of children must be treated alike. This view emerges from both ends of the spectrum, from those who believe that a rigid syllabus and frequent tests of attainment will repair what they regard as the ravages of "modern methods", and from those whose egalitarian sentiments are so compulsive that they would impose an identical restriction on the "high-flier" in the interests of another but equally, or even more, repressive social philosophy.

This chapter has already advanced the view that in relation to children what the adult is has more significance than what he does. Being is more important than doing. A gifted child will certainly be among the first to recognise and respect the knowledge that an adult possesses. But it counts more in his eyes that the adult should have the will and ability to communicate. It is the frankness, sympathy and personal understanding, observed by the pupil in his teacher's being, that puts their relationship on the basis where learning, by one from the other, most readily occurs. When there are one or two children of marked ability in an otherwise average class, the teacher may well have to reconcile conflicts between group and individual relationships. She is concerned not only with the openness of her own stance towards the gifted child, but with the development of social relationships between that child and the rest. A natural tendency on the teacher's part to pay special attention to the ideas and answers of the able child, to commission special jobs from him and even present him as a model to the others, ought to be carefully watched. Undue attention of this kind might well drive a wedge between the gifted child and the rest. It is extremely important that the teacher should be aware of the feeling of the average children towards the child distinguished for his quickness, reliability and brains.

Sometimes such a child is readily and affectionately accepted by the group. He may be known as Dr. Who, "The Brain Box" or "The Professor" and a certain group satisfaction may be derived from the eccentric individuality of his performances. Children may quickly recognise without resentment the natural affinity between one of their kind with these abilities and the teacher. Everything, of course, depends on the personality of the gifted one. Some very able children will seek to dominate their fellows or to humiliate them for their failures. Others may have shy, withdrawing natures. But all will experience the desire to be liked and accepted by their fellows. It is a very exceptional and disturbed child who positively seeks social isolation.

All these are possibilities which the adult will have in mind. To make evident the adult's disposition to aid and understand the individual is a paramount claim, but in schools there is the group, and indeed the whole school community, also existing as equally important entities. The very able child derives from school, like all the rest, certain communal experiences, certain group experiences and certain individual experiences. Ideally his special gifts and powers should be employed and developed in all these three situations.

The teacher's role is to understand the particular abilities and interests of the child and provide what he can to promote their growth. Not all children of marked ability acquire some maturity of outlook and a measure of self-understanding at an early age, but many do. It must not be forgotten that there are qualities, like skill in mathematical calculations, which increase with recognition and practice. The dialogue between the adult and the child rightly changes its tone as maturity increases. It is entirely appropriate that the style and content of conversation between the teacher and the ablest children should be exclusive to their particular relationship. It is not the same relationship as that between the teacher and the dullest child and it would be obscurantist to pretend otherwise. A supposed love and duty towards all children is inappropriately expressed by the neglect or repression of some. Some adults will be as prone to put the quick child in his place as verbally to bully the slow.

In dealing with gifted children nothing is more important than to be frank and truthful. The adult should have no hesitation in revealing the areas of his own ignorance. It should cost him nothing to realise that some children may possess higher intellectual or creative qualities than he does. The differences between individuals, their particular strengths and weaknesses, the difficulties they create for each other, and the help they can give, may all be useful and educative subjects for discussion between adult and child. It is not impossible for a teacher to explain to a pupil what he conceives his function to be and in what ways he is aiming to assist the pupil's development. In response to such advances the bright pupil may find the means of communicating his difficulties or resentments—the boredom he may experience from a routine too unimaginative for his needs, the frustration of feeling his achievements undervalued, the insecurity of his relationship with other children. It is particularly necessary that the child in whom the will to learn burns fiercely should see this passion for knowledge, and delight in the process of enquiry, reflected back from the adults round him.

A normal child has total confidence in his parents because they seem to care for his unique person in a special, all-embracing parental way. Love is then reciprocated and all-powerful whatever happens. A teacher is not a substitute parent, but in all teaching this principle of an established reciprocity can also be applied. The process of education must, as Bruner has observed, be shared with the learner. Teacher and pupil must care not necessarily for each other, but for what they are trying to do, trying to get hold of, trying to make progress towards. There must be created between them some basic harmony of spirit.

After that anything can happen, but all lies in the future. With the very able to fare forward is to contemplate very distant horizons indeed and to assemble the equipment for an endless journey.

CHAPTER IX

In the Primary School

The Plowden Report[1] remains the most substantial and
authoritative document analysing English Primary education
and proposing lines of development for the future. For various
reasons, which need not detain us at this point, the principal
concern of its authors was to initiate reforms which would
benefit the less able child and the children of parents living in
disadvantaged areas. It is not therefore surprising that this
report, exhaustive though it was, had little to say about the
education of unusually able children. Scant attention is afforded
to the problems which arise over children with one very marked
talent; or over children whose general intellectual ability far
surpasses that of parents and neighbours.

There is every evidence of failure in the 1960s to realise that
these were questions of real national importance and not simply
of waste and suffering for individual children. The curious thing
is that the Plowden Committee and its advisers did not seem to
notice the concentration of interest in such questions in the
U.S.A. at the time. Perhaps this neglect is explained by the idio-
syncracies of English educational development. Nothing but a
highly selective system had ever prevailed in English secondary
education, whereas in America the concept of provision for all-
comers had been firmly established, though not always realised.
English primary education had inevitably been influenced by
the distinctive types of secondary provision which existed, both

as a result of historical development and as a matter of deliberate national policy. There was a natural tendency for primary schools to review their pupils in terms of the different kinds of secondary education for which they were being prepared. Certain children of likeable disposition, and with a home background which promoted good social qualities, were expected to achieve educational success. Others seemed not to show the signs that normally aroused teacher expectations of scholastic achievement. Slow learners and slow developers alike were affected by the procrustean bed of the 11+. A lack of encouragement, either from parents or teachers, or both, was clearly a factor that would adversely influence a child's chances of educational success at that early age.

The outstandingly able, however, may well have benefited from the prevalent responses of primary teachers to the selective secondary system. Some successful former pupils have been as loud in their praise of the 11+ oriented primary school as certain old Etonians or Old Summerhillians of their schools. What seems certain, however, is that the supportive home, rich or poor in material things, was a supremely important factor in all but very exceptional cases. When exceptional ability was combined with a reasonably satisfactory home environment, the opportunity of obtaining a highly academic education was open to all in post-war Britain. Highly intelligent parents could be confident that their children, inheriting some measure of their talent, would get an education equal or superior to their own. Only when economic or personal circumstances depressed the conditions of the family as a whole was this unlikely. In the late 1950s such instances were growing fewer.

To this extent then the education of the very able did not cause much anxiety to members of the Councils and Committees on whose advice the Ministers of Education drew. When one reads their names it is apparent that few, if any, could themselves have had children whose gifts were unrecognised or whose education was less full and varied than was appropriate to their level of ability. But among members of the Plowden team there were some individuals who had taught in the ordinary schools of the country where exceptional talent tends to show itself so rarely that in small schools at any rate, few teachers fail to remark it. In the days when H.M. Inspectors were employed to keep in close touch with individual schools, however small and undistinguished, the problems that teachers chose to discuss with these visitors were generally those of their most able and least able pupils. These were the children who attracted notice. The Plowden Report gives some attention to children in the first category, but it amounts to surprisingly little. "The Education of Gifted Children" is one of the shortest of its twenty-nine chapters. Out of 197 final Recommendations only one emerges from the attention that had been given to these children. Long term research studies are suggested and that is hardly a proposal which can have demanded great insight or lengthy discussion.

Of course the Plowden team had to deal with all children in their passage through the Primary Schools. By definition those with exceptional gifts must be but a small proportion of the total. At various points there are indications that the conclusions reached have taken into account the needs and attributes of the "bright" child. It is noted for instance that in project work, children will not be "assimilating inert ideas" but can become "wholly involved in thinking, feeling and doing." The example given is that of a class of seven years olds pursuing an interest in birds which might lead them into the use of reference books, the making of paintings and models, the writing of stories and poems, the construction of a bird table. In such work "the slow and the bright share a common experience and each takes from it what he can at his own level."

To some extent recent discussion of organisation and styles of teaching has been influenced by the problems that arise with those who race ahead of their classmates. This is something that most teachers recognise whether the classes they teach are streamed or unstreamed. It is generally held in the second case that slow children gain from the energy and wider interests of the more able, but the ablest of all may alienate rather than encourage those of below average ability. The brightest children can gain, like all the rest, from individual teaching but the teacher's time is limited. Thus the careful organisation of group teaching is perhaps the most compelling of the primary teacher's tasks. In many schools the whole class is rarely taught together; instead teaching groups are constantly formed and re-formed. It is not always necessary that these groups should be composed of children who share the same classroom base and are placed in the general care of one class teacher.

The principle of setting children to work in relatively small groups can extend across classroom frontiers and can be developed to involve all the teachers in the school and any part-time or ancillary help that may be available. Groups so formed are flexible; the arrangements made are informal, based not on elaborate procedures like tests of general intelligence, but on demonstrated interests, aptitude and sometimes the children's own choice. One thing that clearly emerges when a primary school day is organised in this way is that special abilities are diverse and widely distributed among the children. The lead in group activities does not always come from the same quarter. The existence of bright children and dull children, the quick to read and the slow to read, the physically or artistically adventur-ous and the timid and inept, those with a natural gift for mathematics and those without it, seems to remain unchanged, but there is no longer a rigid stratification of ability or a select group of children on which the teacher's highest expectations always centre.

It is generally accepted that there has been a revolution in English primary school practice within the life time of those of us born in or before the First World War. As in all revolutions there are differences over what has been achieved and what has been destroyed. For the purposes of this book the point at issue must be the effect of change on the progress and attainment of the ablest group of children. Some contemporary expressions of opinion hanker after a return to the past, notably in the direction of more structured styles of learning; but notions of what did take place in the maintained schools, attended by all but a few of the nation's children, are hazy. It would be wise to note what has been written by those who had the best opportuniites of observing those schools in action before making hasty judgements.

As it happens two chief inspectors (HMI) published their life-time impressions directly after their retirement—Edmond Holmes in 1911,[2] John Blackie in 1967.[3] Holmes, with a double first at Oxford behind him, joined the Inspectorate at the age of 25. For twenty years he examined children in the Elementary Schools in accordance with the Code of 1862 under which grants were regulated by reference to the success of children in annual examinations—a system which in his own words "seems to have been devised for the express purpose of arresting growth and strangling life . . . and which had many zealous agents, of whom I, alas! was one."

In the end Holmes[2] analysed with a controlled fury the corrupting effect on elementary school teachers of a situation in which they were forced to drill the pupils into dumb apathy over their part in the scholastic punishment to which fate condemned them. Mechanical reproduction of what had been painfully impressed on their minds was all that the system demanded. What Holmes actually heard in the classrooms of England which he observed for more than thirty years was the endless repetition of such phrases as "Don't talk", "Don't fidget", "Don't ask questions", "Sit still", "Hands on Heads", "Eyes on the Blackboard", "Listen to what I say", "Repeat after me", "Repeat it all together", "Say it three times".

Holmes formed the conviction that such orders and admonitions reflected a total failure to set up the right targets. Education, he decided, was essentially a process of nurturing growth. It was not its purpose to destroy life under the withering crossfire of adult criticism, even though that were to be based on the most high-minded moral or pedagogical principles.

Things changed very slowly as can be seen from Blackie's vivid picture of the primary school as he observed it when he took up his appointment as H.M.I. in 1933.

The children would spend much of the day sitting at double desks or sometimes long desks without backs, and they would either be receiving instruction in the form of class-lessons or be performing tasks of writing, reading or learning by heart. They would seldom, often never, have any opportunity of choosing what they did. Set exercises, set compositions, set books, set drawings or paintings, set music, set physical exercises, set lessons—these dominated most of the day in most schools.

What was it, one is bound to ask, that any child, and particularly the ablest children, are alleged to have gained from such practices, and have now lost as a result of the new departures in primary education? Ignorance joined to prejudice account for much of the hostility towards innovation, and fear of its effects which have been expressed. But not of course all: there have been a number of potent and stimulating criticisms of the ideas and teaching practices which, at an accelerated rate, since the publication of Plowden, seem to be obtaining ascendancy. In so far as they affect the education of the gifted, these criticisms must be given close attention. But first it is important to indicate some of the ways in which brighter children manifestly profit from the freer, more fluid, more enterprising practices of today.

The first is that today's teachers, having themselves been educated more broadly, are encouraged to make the path of a child's education broad rather than narrow. Secondly, despite current set-backs in expenditure, teaching resources, in the shape of books and many other kinds of aids to learning, are infinitely greater. Both these modern developments are immensely advantageous to the able child. He will stand a chance of finding himself encouraged to explore; this means using his intellectual power and (though this is sadly a lesser chance) any other power he may possess, in an active, questing, unconfined manner. The ablest children are those with the greatest ability to judge for themselves, but they are also those most receptive to new suggestions and new materials. The task of the first school with such children is to bring the real things of the world within their reach, to extend the range and enrich the quality of their daily experience.

Prematurely to impose upon them an instruction in skills and techniques, whatever advantage this may have for the less able, is no benefaction to the gifted. It is only necessary to observe such children, to notice their powers of working things out for themselves. Six and seven year olds, endowed with certain attributes, not necessarily those measured by intelligence tests, will persist in their attempts with extraordinary obstinacy. They may express angry scorn for adult aid. Some educationists of today's de-schooling faction seem to believe that all children have innate powers sufficient to set them on the path of self-motivated learning without the need for any adult intervention. This seems at variance with most people's experience, but it is certainly wise that adults, intervening in the self-education of the most able children, should do so very warily indeed. For one thing, those with special gifts may behave in a fashion startling, even incredible, to an adult, unless he has great insight into the child's realms of thought. What quite young children may choose to do can be bewildering, and also exhausting, to the adults around them. Parents and teachers of the gifted may find that it is only common sense to leave them to their own devices at certain times, rather than strive at the impossible task of "putting them on the right lines." An anonymous observer writing more than twenty years ago describes the physical activity of young children in a striking way.[4]

> Children pour all they have into the matter in hand, with no thought of conserving their energy and, because of this, together with their natural agility and lively imagination, they do 'impossible' things in 'impossible' ways. They invent feats unheard of by any adults, they perform antics, climb in ways peculiar to themselves, sit or crouch in outlandish attitudes, tell unlikely tales, act extraordinary characters, and give vent to astonishing noises. It is a time when children explore tirelessly— both their own powers and all that is of interest in their environment; it is also a stage at which they invent, or create, easily and confidently. It seems important that children should be allowed to enjoy this stage to the full.

A greater freedom of movement and a greater freedom of speech may therefore be two of the ways in which modern educational practice serves young and gifted children better than the old

J

ways. A freer access to books and the much greater encouragement given to reading by relating it to centres of interest set up
in the child's own mind, with or without teacher intervention, is
clearly another advantage. Success in making the school as a
whole a place in which the curiosity of a child is stimulated
has a special value for the more able. Collections of interesting
objects, natural and man-made, materials for construction of
various kinds—all such things, nowadays to be found in a great
many schools, attract the attention and stimulate the ingenuity
of pupils. In themselves they can as well suggest activities,
experiments, quests for knowledge, as the positive proposals or
directions of a teacher. Time to continue uninterrupted the
investigation of a problem or the completion of a chosen task is
now a normal concession. For the more gifted this is indeed a
bonus.

Recognition of the importance of attention to the "developmental" as opposed to the chronological age of the child is
likely to improve the educational prospects of the gifted. This
concept of developmental age has stemmed from some highly
influential research—that of Jean Piaget who has sought to
identify clear landmarks in the growth of a child's thought
processes. Each stage of its development brings the possibility
of acquiring new powers and new skills within the child's grasp.
But all depends on an adequate attainment at each of the earlier
stages. A child does not learn to walk before he has learned to
stand, and whether dull or bright must acquire the ability to
discriminate shapes before learning to read. All this has influenced primary teachers in the direction of less rigid regard to
the chronological age of children, and more concern with
individual stages of growth. The treatment of gifted children as
well as those with learning difficulties has unquestionably been
improved as a result.

The Plowden Committee speculated on whether it would be
useful to lay down standards of achievement for primary schools
and came to the conclusion that such an aim was impossible to
achieve. Much discussion and considerable private and public
anxiety has centred on this question of standards in recent years.

No one disputes the need for recording children's educational progress and evaluating the work of schools. But the view of the Plowden Report that "any set standard would seriously limit the bright child and be impossibly high for the dull" would still command the support of most teachers and probably of most parents. In spite of grave lapses, to which public attention has been drawn from time to time, there is substantial confidence in the achievements of English primary education. The parents of exceptional children contribute as much or more to this feeling as do the parents of those of average capacity. It is the very absence of rigidity and narrow constraint that serves the needs of able children best. All parents who have attempted to educate their own gifted child, and all the evidence of those conducting "enrichment" programmes for such children, confirm this.

It is not difficult to note aspects of English primary education which give rise to public concern and where reforms are needed, but that minority section of the community interested in the early education of gifted children should be the very last to clamour for a return to the past. One of the main objectives of those most active in the study of early childhood learning is that the work of the schools should be more personal, more individual, more expertly structured to meet the varying needs of children. These are precisely the conditions under which the more able are likely to flourish. This assertion, obvious enough to those who care at first hand for such children, is not always acceptable either to the public at large or to some teachers of older children.

The opinion is sometimes advanced that the freer, child-centred exploratory type of learning may be well-suited to the able child of middle-class origin with good backing from home, but that these modern ways ill serve the able child from the working-class with lesser home support. This is not an argument that can be lightly dismissed. There are subjects like mathematics, and also language and literature, both our own and that of other countries, where teaching in the secondary school will be more difficult, if structure and sequence has been neglected in the primary school years. Mathematical apparatus and games, good standards of speech, praise and encouragement of reading and writing attainment may compensate for such weaknesses, but these advantages are less likely to come the way of the culturally deprived in "poor" areas except from the teachers and the schools. Poor areas in this respect can be found in cities, suburbs and the country. To impose tests of attainment on these schools where the early processes of education are already prejudiced by home conditions would do no one any good and have dire effects on the education of the abler child. Such steps would further depress the readiness of teachers to undertake two of the most difficult but most important of their tasks. The first of these is the promotion of effective oral work and the second the setting-up of situations from which children can grasp some of those concepts on which an understanding of mathematics depends. The importance of good early teaching in language and mathematics and the recently developed ideas on what constitutes such teaching are matters with which, in the first case the Bullock Report *A Language for Life*[5] deals in great detail, and which in the second is expounded in the widely read work by Miss Edith Biggs, written when she was one of H.M. Staff Inspectors for Mathematics.[6]

The question that must interest readers of this book is whether children of pronounced, if not exceptional, ability, are as "advanced" in their reading and mathematical attainment at the ages of 7, 9 and 11 as were children of similar ability twenty, thirty or forty years ago. Even if it could be proved of such children (one in 8 to one in 10 of the whole child population) that they did less well than their predecessors at 7 or 9, this would be of no concern if it could also be shown that at 11 or 14 they had caught up. Unfortunately it is very difficult to prove anything in this area of smouldering controversy. In the absence of statistical evidence it is reasonable to consider the views of the most widely experienced observers. What did happen to primary mathematics in the reform era of the 1950s and 1960s? Almost certainly nothing that could have had the slightest adverse effect on the attainment of the able pupil. In the opinion of Edith

Biggs, pupils working along the new lines, under teachers who understood what they were doing, covered more mathematics than in the past, and that "provided the teachers gave them systematic practice in computation there is no loss of efficiency. . . ."

The Plowden Report explained and summarised the principles underlying the new approach. It expressed the view that ample evidence supported the reforms, that it was unnecessary to fear that computation would be given too little attention, and that in any case the impending introduction of the decimal system would reduce the time necessary for arithmetical calculation. "The third of the three Rs is no longer mere mechanical arithmetic . . . The gloomy forebodings of the decline of knowledge which would follow progressive methods have been discredited." Further evidence, particularly significant in the context of the gifted child, may be found in the elaborate international evaluation of achievement in mathematics completed in 1967 under the guiding influence of Professor Husen.[8] The crude scores recorded by the various national samples of secondary school students put England into second place (behind Israel) in this contest. Even when allowance was made for our selective system which provided a small population from which our students were drawn, much smaller than, for instance, the U.S.A., it was still clear that English standards in mathematics were relatively very high. Our ablest young mathematicians seemed to have been taught at least as well as those in any other country; this has been confirmed by performances in the International Mathematical Olympiades which have subsequently taken place.

Notwithstanding these results the demand for an evaluation of attainment in mathematics was increasingly pursued. It led eventually at the request of the D.E.S. to the N.F.E.R's efforts to carry out a national survey. The important thing about this work is that it seems effectively to have broken up the subject into measurable parts. No one can say whether school mathematics as a whole is improving or deteriorating. But it could be shown, as a result of tests given to children at 11 + and at 15 +, that performance on questions which revealed ability to deal with sets had improved and with calculations had deteriorated. This may be a national disaster if the capacity to calculate of junior employees in offices and factories is really as important as occasional angry letters to the newspapers suggest, but it is obviously to the advantage of the gifted child and probably also to the future state of the national economy.

The evidence about standards of attainment in the language arts and skills is easier to examine because it is surveyed in the Bullock Report. Lord Bullock's committee also carried out an important piece of research based on questionnaires completed by nearly 2000 schools. In this primary teachers were asked to give a rating for reading ability of 6 and 9 year old children within the sample. The teachers were asked first to assume that 25% were good readers for their age, 50% average and 25% poor readers, but they actually placed 30·8% of six year olds and 41% of nine year olds in the first category. Were they over-rating the ability in particular of the nine year olds or did they mean what they said? When secondary teachers were asked in the same terms to rate 14-year-olds, only 26·4% were placed in the top category. A not improbable explanation of these figures is that primary teachers really do monitor the reading progress of nine year olds very closely, whereas those dealing with fourteen year olds had not themselves been responsible for teaching reading and were therefore less inclined to draw fine distinctions between individual children. Nowhere in the Report is anything to be found that would sustain the contention that gifted children are handicapped by the methods used for language teaching in primary schools, even though, as the Report asserts, the gap in reading attainment between the most able and the least able has narrowed.

The Bullock Committee of enquiry was even more reticent about gifted children than the Central Advisory Council under Lady Plowden's chairmanship. Once again it would appear that distinguished people, educationists and others alike, found in their personal experience support for the conventional judgement that gifted children were bound to succeed without any special attention being given to their needs. The Bullock survey showed that nearly half the ablest six year old readers read to their teachers only occasionally (less than three times a week). More than half the ablest nine year olds seem never to read to their teachers at all, and about a third of them only once a week. These returns did not cause the committee any disquiet. Nor did the evidence it received about the growth of mixed ability grouping for the teaching of English in middle schools and the early years of secondary schools. The committee was apparently divided on the question of streaming or setting for English. The majority appeared to be hostile to these practices—or at least to have reservations about them, but one such reservation is distinctly odd—"the fact that it would steadily deprive the more able of opportunities to communicate with the linguistically less accomplished." Applied to Physics it would certainly be a strange notion that disaster might attend the abler student if denied the opportunity of communicating with those who knew nothing or cared little about the subject.

The main point against mixed ability grouping in English for children of this age was well put to the Committee by at least one witness. It is the simple fact that reading ability will vary in such a group and consequently there will be a wide divergence in maturity of interests and taste. Feelings for style and quality will have grown up in some children and be totally absent in others, who may still be struggling to master the mechanics of reading. The almost inevitable strategy for the teacher in such a situation is to ignore all aspects of the subject in which more searching questions might be raised, and thus to prevent any divergence of reading level from showing itself. Improvised dramatisation, so-called creative writing and chatty discussions do very well for this purpose. The abler child of the 1970s will be as bored, and as ill-served, by these activities as was the abler child in the elementary school of the 1870s by the monotony of spelling drill. Both that practice and mixed ability grouping must have appeared in some way excusable as being conducive to the health of society, however unpleasant for the individual.

It is true that one member of the Bullock Committee, a junior school headmaster, made points similar to these in a dissenting statement appended to the Report. Unfortunately his judgements seem somewhat clouded by the old-world romanticism of opinions he had expressed on mathematics.[9] "Arithmetic had had always been from the earliest days of the elementary system one of the most loved and popular periods on the time-table. Nothing in school is quite as satisfying to a teacher as a page of sums neatly done and just as neatly ticked or crossed in red pencil. For the child, a sum-book full of gloriously correct examples, each with its little blazon for achievement, was a possession to be prized."

One might hazard a guess that the author of such a passage had little notion of what gifted children can do or of the kind of teacher likely to promote their best interests.

Romantics à la Rousseau, and lovers of myth, are of course to be found on both sides of the great divide between modern and traditional styles of primary education. "Only a romantic pedagogue," writes J. S. Bruner,[10] "would say that the main object of schooling is to preserve the child's intuitive gift. And only a foolish one would say that the principal object is to get him beyond all access to intuition, to make a precise analytic machine of him. Obviously the aim of a balanced schooling is to enable the child to proceed intuitively when necessary and to analyse when appropriate." Many modern teachers are convinced (and in Bruner's opinion rightly so) that the traditional role of the teacher as the one who knows, and can therefore settle by means of tick or cross the open question of what the pupil knows, has to be abandoned. A teacher must practise the speculative strategies of one who seeks after knowledge *and* the firm stance of one who in certain circumstances constitutes a knowledge-model for his pupils. For what the able child, even of junior school age, looks for is the opportunity freely to try out his own intuitive powers *and* to consult a model which actually works. To watch an intelligent child at grips with a constructional kit provides an immediate understanding of this point. Both the child's own experimental approach and the instruction provided are vital to success. To quote Bruner again —"for complex activity to be brought off intelligently it must have a sequential pattern such that the whole is kept in mind while the parts are strung together."

The children with which this book is concerned are those who manifest an interest in learning. This may be so obsessive an interest that they become in fact difficult to teach. The obsession of bright children may for instance centre so exclusively on one particular thing, about which there is much to learn, that they have literally no time for anything else which teachers and parents may consider it important that they should master. Under the influence first of John Dewey, and then of his many disciples, the idea has been spread that children's interests should lie at the roots of all true learning. Without contesting that supposition one can see that it has only limited value as a practical guide to teaching. It is particularly dubious to apply the children's-interests principle to the education of those of high ability. The devouring curiosity that consumes them tends to create a vast range of interests and so leads to restlessly diffused activity. At the other extreme it may restrict itself to one all-absorbing but narrow interest, so obsessive that it excludes attention to all sorts of other important things. One set of important things which children need to get from early education are precise skills and positive attitudes to learning.

In a good primary school teachers will have made up their own minds which of the many needs that children have, and which of the many interests they may show, are going to be satisfied and developed by the agency of the school. The school has to act appropriately and with competence. Teachers have idealised aims and some knowledge of the practical steps necessary to realise them. They must at first win from the children a free acceptance of the disciplines implicit in the attainment of these ends. Discipline in this sense implies some sort of orderly and purposeful management of one's energy. It is for instance impossible to learn to read without a disciplined control over the movements of the eye. A part of the order demanded by intellectual activity is physical, and a part of that demanded by a physical activity, such as dancing or rock-climbing, is mental. It is beyond the teacher's power to order, or even to instruct, a child to read or to dance. What she can do is to control the arrangements which must necessarily be made before reading or dancing can take place. These are not of course simply physical arrangements—not merely the flash-cards, the book, the music, the uncluttered open-space. They extend to control over the child's energies and over the way the mind of the child is used. The proper exertion of these controls takes time and depends on so shaping the attitudes of the children that the structured procedures necessary to learning are readily acceptable.

The argument of this chapter has been that primary school methods, recommended by the Plowden Report and by most authorities on early childhood education, are on the whole well-suited to the more able members of the school population. Rigidity and restriction implicit in a syllabus tightly controlled by periodic testing, in fact a return to the past in any shape or form, would do us grave disservice.

Able children thrive in the open country of learning: they must have freedom of movement or their impulses to obtain knowledge will slowly atrophy. The concentrated energy with which some young children pursue their ends can be blighted by the imposition of too rigid or too narrow a mode of teaching. Unimaginative teaching is indeed one of the principal reasons why some able children do less well than would be expected. An input-output model for primary education, the tight prescription of certain skills which must be learned at all cost, could be worth considering in the case of very dull pupils. It would have nothing to offer those of average competence and could be positively disastrous to the most able.

There is much to be admired in English primary education, but there are weaknesses, and they tend to bear heavily on the ablest children. Often the power structure in the school – the way it is organised and managed – is inimical to these children's interests. The education and later the professional training of the many primary teachers leaves them a long way from posses-

sing the confidence needed to teach the ablest groups, let alone
the necessary knowledge and imagination.

It could never be easy to assemble clear-cut evidence to
support a critical view of primary education. We can only go on
what experienced informed observers find wanting when they
visit the schools. Also worth consideration are the motives
which sometimes lead parents to remove a child from the
maintained primary school and place him in an independent
school. Here an interesting two-way process is in operation
which might repay study. Some parents of bright children, who
have started early in the private sector, are happy to move them
later into a maintained school, while others reverse the process.
Generally their reason for doing so seems to be the slow pace
and unexacting scholastic standards of the particular primary
school.

The Bullock Committee concluded that it was false to assert
that attention to the basic skills in language was neglected. Yet
on occasion relatively casual remarks in its Report are sufficiently alarming. For instance this—"We talked to teachers who
never read a story or a poem to the class or talked to the
children collectively. Indeed some felt that they would be wrong
to teach the class or any part of it directly, since this would
compromise their commitment to a 'child-centred' programme."
When this position is adopted in relation to a junior class as a
whole, it is the ablest children who suffer most. But of course
other absurd dogmas, occasionally encountered, such as the
alleged immorality of keeping records or the irrelevance of
teaching a child to write, cast their shadows on the average and
below average. There is an overwhelming weight of evidence
that all children's progress in language arts and skills and in
mathematical understanding, is directly related to well-planned
and well-organised schemes of work. No less important are
careful records of each child's attainments and weaknesses. The
absence of structure in the work, the neglect of routine checking,
the activity as a target in itself with no relation to what the
children might learn by it, a general sloppiness associated with
underestimating the children's potential—these are all clear signs

of what can go wrong, largely because certain aspects of the philosophy underlying modern educational development are misunderstood. An experienced school visitor who has done as much as any chief education officer to foster the revolution in primary schools has made this point plainly. "When a class seems happy but is totally lacking in purpose it is no answer for the teacher to say with a warning smile 'Ah, but we are doing a project', or 'All our work is open-ended' or worse still, as one teacher put it, 'We are a muck and muddle school but we are all happy'. In such schools when the work is lamentably undemanding the effect as one visitor put it is that of a wet play time all day."

When, in a subject such as mathematics, a long accepted structure is toppled by theories or events, the results are by no means uniform or predictable. Three different areas in Wales were recently studied by H.M. Inspectors[12] who were interested to discover who was responsible for the schemes of work in each case. When the teaching of mathematics is affected by new ideas, methods and materials, it seems necessary that teachers should have some general framework within which to work, especially when very few have themselves studied mathematics beyond O-level. In one area a scheme prepared by the L.E.A.'s adviser in mathematics was available to teachers. In the second, where an 11+ mathematics examination still obtained, the teaching was naturally geared to this, following a syllabus produced in co-operation with the secondary school specialists. These schemes provided teachers with a balanced programme of work, often supplemented in individual schools by notes on organisations' and lists of books, work cards and equipment. In the third area some heads held the view that written guidance might have a restrictive influence on the teachers' freedom. The result was that in most schools there were no schemes or guidelines and in them the work was found to be mainly text-book-based, more restricted and stereotyped than where expert suggestion had been made available.

Another example of the need for attention to structure can be found in a study by H.M. Inspectors of junior school geography.[13] Carefully thought-out attempts were made to examine the way pupils acquired their knowledge and to judge attainment in the subject. In the majority of the schools studied, geography was not given a separate identity but was absorbed into combined studies under various titles. In the inspectors' judgement the standards of work, and levels of achievement in what would be accounted as geographical knowledge, were not adversely affected by this. In fact the most successful geography was found in schools which gave the subject recognition within a combined studies programme. On the other hand poor schemes of work, the total absence of schemes and general inattention to planning were adjudged the main causes of failure. Of the schools which had an adequate scheme of work 77% produced good or moderately good results. Of the schools with no schemes only 40% produced work of any quality.

It is all too seldom realised that the ablest children may reject or resist the standard approach of the school just as much as do the least able. The range of their interests, the speed of their understanding, their capacity to extend and elaborate their enterprises, using flights of imagination and degrees of intelligence unfamiliar to their teachers, all demand attention. It is too rarely provided either in the work set them or in the materials, including books, available for their use. There are too many books and pictures of poor quality, too few globes, maps, charts, diagrams, sand trays, working models, tape recorders. The ablest children will not be content with inconsequent fragments of knowledge; they should be exercised in logical thinking: they should be given encouragement to formulate and test their own hypotheses.

In reading and general language development it is seldom that special attention is given to the more able and yet the whole point of breaking up the class unit is to secure assignments suited to ability, group interaction amongst the children and teacher intervention to meet individual needs. The able children should have opportunities for oral discussion of topics in which they take an interest. There ought to be occasions when they can hear stories, poems or other readings of a quality calculated to extend their powers of understanding. They should have practice in reading aloud to achieve real standards of clarity, mood and feeling. They should be encouraged to achieve self-expression in improvised dramatisations and to develop their powers of reasoning in debate with others whose logical sense is equally advanced.

Children highly gifted in music will probably have been picked out before reaching the age of 11 for special attention. Parents can see for themselves how positive and compelling is the attraction that music has for a certain boy or girl. The support that many primary schools receive from music advisers, peripatetic teachers of music or musical friends and parents goes far to ensure that the musical child's special gift is not neglected. It is by no means as clear that the child who is drawn towards language, science or mathematics, with the same inner compulsion shown by musical children, will be given extended exercise in the use of his or her talent. The special aptitudes of such children for science or language learning may not even be recognised for what they are. The teaching of science in primary schools is haphazard and very much dependent on the fortuitous interests and abilities of individual teachers, some of whom, it must be said, do remarkable things.

What happened to the teaching of French in primary schools is an object lesson. Until the 1960s it was assumed that only the more able children would profit from beginning to learn a foreign language as early as the age of eight. Some schools however, favoured in the lottery of staffing, had interesting results to show from experiments in teaching French to whole groups. There followed a large and protracted national project to test out the feasibility of introducing French to all children. Teachers were trained for the work; course materials were specially prepared; pilot schools were selected in thirteen different areas of the country, and many other primary schools elected to join in, using the same teaching materials. The working of this expensive and elaborate scheme was intensively studied both by H.M. Inspectors and in a highly sophisticated research project carried out by the National Foundation for

Educational Research.[14] The conclusions drawn were deeply disappointing, particularly in respect of the attitude shown by the children concerned. The starry-eyed belief that all children would enjoy and profit from French was confounded by the facts. Most children (boys in particular) were bored, confused, disheartened and even contemptuous. Too often the freedom with which heads control their allocation of time, rooms and staffing resources produced conditions that ruled out successful teaching and also the possibility of continuity extending into the secondary school. The audio-visual methods and even the materials were not always understood. Some of the work attempted was manifestly counter-productive.

There is now no serious dispute about the teaching of French to all in primary schools regardless of ability. It cannot be done. This makes it all the more important to remember that the most able children should not be denied the opportunity of starting a foreign language early in precisely the same way that a child with a talent for music should not be denied access to a piano. Learning a language and a musical instrument are generally held to demand daily practice or something as near to this as possible. In very few primary schools would this be attainable. It is only therefore to be expected that the parents of able children with linguistic gifts are going to be increasingly anxious and disturbed about the apparent incapacity of maintained primary schools to offer them a sufficiently challenging approach to our own language or any opportunities commensurate with their ability in a foreign language.

Under the old regime in post-war primary schools of more than one form entry streaming was the normal practice. Expectations were formed on which a scholarship or 11+ group was taken through the process considered necessary to ensure that a proportion at least of the children it contained would be allocated to a grammar school. Groups regarded as slower to learn, less responsive to the pressures required for examination success were set different objectives. Teacher opinion, in recent years, has swung strongly against such general arrangements. One result has been that the ablest children are now less easily identified in the primary school. Another probability is that the best teaching the school provides is not so exclusively concentrated on the ablest children. The mistakes made in selection for secondary education were due more often than has been realised to the variation of size of primary schools. Great numbers of them were too small for any kind of streaming, and so staffed that undue concentration of resources on those with the best prospect of grammar school entry was impossible, even had it been desired. The changing attitude of teachers towards their work, the new concepts of individualised learning, the scope given to able children to exercise their own initiative and sometimes their own imagination and creative sense—all were factors which more than compensated the ablest children for any disadvantage which the new ways of working might have brought.

Streamed primary schools are neither desirable nor practicable today. What then is the effect of this on the ablest children? It is not catastrophic but it is somewhat disquieting; though it may be no more than one child in 18 or 20 with whom we are here concerned, the personal and social importance of that child's education is far-reaching. The objection to streaming has in many cases been associated with a bland, often sentimental belief that if all children are treated alike they will all do equally well. To turn a blind eye to evidence of exceptional talent saves a teacher the task of preparing and supervising individual work suited to high ability; and this can be a very demanding task indeed.

The child with a very marked special ability can be given certain opportunities out of school. Various special afternoon or Saturday morning arrangements and early evening teaching of for instance a musical instrument often do what the school itself cannot or will not do for the very gifted. But there are vastly greater numbers of young children whose abilities are only partially recognised. There are the children, equally distributed throughout the population, as far as we know, whose minds are so made that intellectual discipline and a certain academic rigour suit them well. Their growth and development as people may depend on these factors as much as the musical child's development depends on musical opportunity. In many cases parents and adult friends and relatives compensate such children for the fact that their primary school offers them too little challenge and too narrow a range of interests, often just trivial substitutes for the real thing— especially perhaps in literature and science.

The sad thing is that many such children do not experience the stimulus and support of adults outside the school. They will get what they can from the ubiquitous TV receiver, perhaps. It is a poor replacement for the life and warmth of human contact. For the gifted child, at the level at which he craves it, there may be less chance of this than there used to be in the days of the 11 + and the "scholarship" class. Fewer primary teachers today seem to feel that their soul is lifted by the response of the child whose lively interest in life distinguishes him from the rest. Or else they have been taught a stern repression. More important than abstract ideas about equality is what D. H. Lawrence wrote,[15] so sharply and accurately, about Paul Morel. He was of course describing himself and at the same time many other bright children of the working class.

> Usually he looked as if he saw things, was full of life and warm . . . . and then, when there was any clog in his soul's quick running, his face went stupid and ugly. He was the sort of boy that becomes a clown and a lout as soon as he is not understood, or feels himself held cheap; and again is adorable at the first touch of warmth. He suffered very much from the first contact with anything. When he was seven, the starting school had been a nightmare and a torture to him. But afterwards he liked it.

The vital aim in primary education today is how to foster a proper concern for standards without prejudice to the more varied and imaginative teaching styles which so many schools have themselves developed. Failure to resolve this difficulty will be profoundly detrimental to the more able children.

K

CHAPTER X

In the Secondary School

In primary education instances of conflict between traditionalists and innovators are naturally to be found. The quality of the schools, however, seems to depend less on the outcome of such conflict and more on the confidence and stability of the staff. What teachers actually do affects the children more than what they believe. In secondary schools these factors emerge as even more decisive because in some urban areas a stable school staff has been almost impossible to achieve. Furthermore such schools have often to offer family social services before they are in a position to meet the educational needs of individual children. It is useless to demand high academic standards of all secondary schools when there are many that have mainly to concentrate on the simplest physical and intellectual skills, combining this with trying to transmit socially acceptable attitudes and styles of behaviour.

A grave disservice has been done to secondary education by attempts to impose uniform rigid orthodoxies on the type of school to be established and the aims to be pursued. It was greatly to the credit of the comprehensive school reformers in the 1960s that a variety of secondary school development was encouraged and a relatively realistic pace of growth envisaged. The nation enjoyed the good fortune to have in office at a critical time as flexible and imaginative a minister as the late Mr Crosland. Political warfare over the structure of the secondary school might otherwise have taken a heavier toll than it has so far done.

Nevertheless there are some indications that able children, perhaps girls in particular, have suffered educational disadvantage from recent developments. This suggestion would certainly be disputed and is difficult to prove. Even if a regression from the standards achieved in the past were admitted, it would still have to be recognised that a comparatively small proportion of the school population is all that could be affected; and that small number affected only in certain ways. Later we must try to identify the disadvantages which able children tend to suffer in many of today's secondary schools.

It is important to appreciate that the actual variations in maintained schools for older children are very great both in England and the U.S.A. where decentralized systems of provision are firmly entrenched. On both sides of the Atlantic there is no uniformity in those institutions which bridge the gap between elementary (child) education and entry into work, or into higher (adult) education as the English would put it. Not all secondary schools have the same kind of strengths or the same kind of weaknesses. The effects of secondary schools on the education of the able may be as variable as the schools themselves. But certain things are common to all the newer comprehensive secondary schools. They do not possess traditions and they are bound to accommodate a wider range of abilities than has been common in English secondary schools. In some areas too they are required to teach a greater number of the children of recent immigrants than ever before in the past.

Some of the earlier ideas about the planning of comprehensive schools have had to be qualified or abandoned; most notably the belief that such schools ought to be very large whenever the distribution of population made this possible. The main reason for supposing that the new comprehensives must be bigger than the old secondary grammar or modern school was provided by the concept of the viable sixth form. Unless a large range of subjects could be offered to the older pupils, it was believed that they would leave school prematurely and the new comprehensive would fail to present the public with a reasonable alternative to the old grammar school. The assumptions generally made were that a sixth form of 80 to 100 students required a supporting base of at least 900, that is to say six forms of 30 over a period of five years. It therefore became the object of most local education authorities, who wanted to provide all-though comprehensives for the age range 11 to 18, to plan for schools of not less than 1,000 pupils in any circumstances. Many planned and brought into operation very much larger schools. In London it seemed that numbers between 2,000 and 2,500 were appropriate and in cities such as Bristol 1,500 to 1,800.

The point can be illustrated by contrasting a fairly typical mixed grammar school as it was in 1974 with a new comprehensive school under another authority but not very distant. The grammar school was by no means a highly selective institution. 30% of the area's child population entered it at 11. The social background was naturally varied and academic expectations were not especially high. The staffing ratio was virtually identical to that of the comprehensive. Out of 882 pupils, 130 were taking two or more A-levels, 26 one A-level. The new comprehensive school drew its pupils from a massive corporation housing estate. It had 1,560 on its roll of whom 77 were taking two A-levels and 39 one A-level. In order to have a sixth form sufficiently large to offer a range of subjects without gross extravagance in staffing, and to assemble together enough able pupils to provide competitive stimulus, it was necessary for the comprehensive school to be nearly twice as large as the grammar school, and even then in this case the potential university candidates were twice as numerous in the grammar school.

To understand why in England the question of providing for the top 10% of the school came to rule judgements about the size of school appropriate also for the other 90%, it is necessary to understand the traditional framework of the most respected English grammar schools. The thing to realise is that they conducted two quite distinct and separate courses—one for the School Certificate, later the O-level examination of the General Certificate of Education to be taken not later than age 16, and one for the Higher Certificate, later the A-level, which began at about 16 and in two or possibly three years prepared students for entry to university or professional training. If the secondary modern school could have been staffed and equipped to offer a fair proportion of its pupils O-level opportunities, there would not perhaps have been so strong an eventual disapproval of the selective secondary system as established in 1944. Maintained grammar schools might then have become establishments where pupils took O-levels in their stride, if they took them at all, and concentrated all their attention on the upper school course to A-level. They would have shrunk in number, but might have provided exemplary service to the academically minded ten per cent, without incurring any opprobium at all on grounds of "elitism" or "divisive" influence. Ever increasing numbers of parents were concerned about their children's chances of success at O-level, but relatively few about A-levels.

In pointing out the educational advantages of the then new G.C.E. examination, the Ministry of Education Pamphlet (1950) stressed the restrictive nature of the old School Certificate which it was to replace. This was a class examination though not in a Marxist sense. It had been designed when state secondary education was in its infancy to test the school as a whole in respect of the performances produced by complete classes of pupils. The effect was to depress the freedom of teachers to develop individual work and the initiative of their more able fifth form pupils. The new examination on the contrary would "follow the line of a pupil's natural developments, being planned in terms of his whole school life." A course terminating at the age of 16 provided nothing but "the illusion of a completed education." The view of the Ministry's experts, the H.M.I.'s of that era, was clear enough and quite uncompromising about academic standards and what was necessary to achieve them. In the case of able pupils, that is those whose aim would be A-level success in two or three subjects, it was recommended that they should not take their main subjects at O-level. Instead they should concentrate from the beginning upon a steady and un-broken progress to their ultimate objective. The less able should

not in their own interests be put in for formal academic examinations, but for an internal test, covering what they *had* been
able to do rather than what had been left undone.

The question of school size turned out to be vitally affected by
logistics. It became clear that only when an entirely new building
had been erected was it possible to assemble the numbers of
pupils who, if there was no selection by ability, required to be
educated together in order to achieve a sizeable sixth form and
with it the prestige of the grammar school. Progress towards a
comprehensive system as a replacement for the old selective
system had necessarily to be slow. But those who objected
strongly to selection at 11 grew impatient. Two local education
authorities, the West Riding of Yorkshire and the County of
Leicestershire, took the lead in a break away from the original
London concept of an all-in 11–18 school, based on the high
schools of New York and Indiana, which Sir Graham Savage
(later Chief Education Officer to the London County Council)
had studied in 1925 when he was an H.M.I. The only possible
escape from logistical bonds lay in the devising of a two-tier
pattern of schools and this in the early 1960s was attempted by
the authorities mentioned above and later by some others. In
such a system all who left the primary school went first to a
middle school or junior comprehensive secondary school and at
13 or 14 were transferred to a comprehensive high school, or at
16 were transferred either to the sixth form college, recruiting
at that age, or to the sixth form of an all-through school.

Early in the evolution of comprehensive secondary education
it became clear to the public in all but the most rural areas that
the new schools would differ from the old in at least one respect.
They would be much larger. There was also an increasing likelihood that instead of being, at least in theory, 11–18 schools
many of them would fall into one of the other admissible
categories listed in the government's circular which in 1965
called on local authorities to prepare plans for establishing
comprehensive schools. Thus the point of entry to the secondary
school, the need for transfer to another school at a later stage,
the opportunity of pursuing General Certificate courses at O

and A level were all subject to regional variation. It was not easy for a parent to foresee in a system reorganised on comprehensive lines the same clear pattern of opportunity within a single institution that his child would have had if he or she had obtained entry to the grammar school of the past. Here then was one respect in which the ablest children from the less well endowed homes were handicapped by change.

In other directions the early comprehensive schools proceeded to plant their progressive feet in the track of the grammar school. The first generation heads tended to adopt various grammar school practices. Prefects, a "house" system, school uniform and selective streaming were common features taken over from the schools to which prestige had traditionally attached. For as many pupils as possible syllabuses of work were geared to the same external examinations as the grammar schools' pupils had attempted. If this was impracticable then at least all possible candidates could be entered for the less prestigious Certificate of Secondary Education. The established boundaries and defence systems of the main academic subjects were preserved. Thus the senior teachers in charge of mathematics, science or modern languages throughout the school were in positions of great authority. The separate subjects from which a balanced curriculum could be constructed formed the foundation of the curriculum in the middle years. After that specialisation, on one side or the other of the traditional arts and sciences divide, was the normal practice for those of academic ability. Indifference to the idea of careers education and to the introduction of expertise in counselling or careers guidance, a characteristic feature of the grammar school, was almost as marked in the early comprehensives. The secondary modern school was shown by the careers education survey of 1972 to be far more likely to include such an innovation in the fourth year curriculum than comprehensive or grammar schools.[2]

It could certainly be argued that some comprehensive schools, by taking the grammar school as a model, created many difficulties for themselves. Others, however, now seem to have moved too fast and too far in a precisely opposite direction. In order to distribute resources equitably in an all-range-of-ability school, it became inevitable that targets should be less distant (it took seven years to become a grammar school "success"). With the same object in view the attention of the most able teaching began to be diverted from the most able pupils towards the rest. Teachers themselves tended to be less preoccupied with the tasks of imparting knowledge and introducing their pupils to practise and perfect certain forms of skill. They sought instead to act as advisers, organisers and production agents with a first duty of acquiring or creating the materials from which their pupils were to learn. To compile a work sheet which might guide the pupil to an understanding of scientific or mathematical principles was often a more valued teacher activity than the conventional discourse, demonstration and questioning. The new aims are clearly put by the Principal and Deputy Principal of the Abraham Moss Centre in Manchester. This is a significant large-scale development of the community college idea pioneered by Henry Morris in Cambridgeshire. It includes a two-tier (but not separate) comprehensive school, a college of further education, together with arts, sports, adult education and club provision for young and old. Writing in 1977 it is difficult to imagine such a grandiose experiment ever being repeated.

> The essential need is for a major shift towards the creation of a learning environment in which the pupils are not entirely dependent upon the teacher for their learning. Instead individual pupils are provided with structured materials at their level of understanding, which they are able to approach and work on independently of the teacher, who is still available to work with them, providing encouragement and stimulation, helping where problems arise, and keeping a close watch on their progress. This would not be to the exclusion of a whole range of other experiences, from being part of a large or small group listening and watching, taking part in some activity, working or discussing together, or being guided or tutored by a teacher.

Provided that good foundations have been laid in the lower school (11–13) there is no reason why the more able children should not be well-served by such a style of teaching. Unfortunately there are doubts about what can be achieved in mixed ability classes of eleven or twelve year olds, especially in a district where the general level of regard for intellectual and cultural pursuits is not high. Amongst children whose expectations of school life do not extend beyond the statutory years, whose attitude to abstractions is negative, whose mental and artistic horizons are confined, the individual with high intelligence, insight, curiosity or creative power, especially if that individual is a girl in a mixed school, is seldom happily situated. The balance is tilted against her prospects as a potential high performer, whatever the main field of interest to which she is drawn, and especially if this should chance to be physics, chemistry or mathematics. But more serious than this is the general atmosphere of hostility and indifference to things of the mind, to basic elements in the manner of life of those who want to study and so to diversify their contacts with life. In anti-intellectual societies, those who pursue unfamiliar and distant goals are unacceptable to the rest. Good foundations at the first stage of secondary school organisation depend less on organisational factors, such as banding, streaming, or mixed ability grouping, less on curriculum content—a foreign language, separate science subjects or general science—and much more on the recognised standards of working relationships between pupil and pupil and between pupil and teacher. Unless these are orderly, tolerant and mutually respectful, classroom conditions are bound to have an adverse effect on learning. The will and the ability of the teacher to exercise firm but friendly supervision and control at this stage, is of supreme importance. Its absence prejudices the education of all, including the most able, but more especially, it reduces the educational prospects of those whose home situations afford them little or no encouragement.

·Restlessness, noise, damage and disruptive violence, more often verbal than physical, has undoubtedly increased in the early and middle stages of secondary education. These unhappy things have come to be associated with the large urban comprehensive schools. Heads have naturally been reluctant to expose these tendencies, but at least two young heads in Inner London

have had the courage to do so publicly. One wrote soon after
taking over the headship of a mixed secondary school:

> The ravages of a recent history of staff turnover, staff shortages
> in key departments and a resultant parade of supply teachers
> (described as the 'plimsoll brigade' by a more experienced
> colleague) had left a considerable mark on both staff and pupils . . .
> Clearly some teachers will achieve more than others, especially
> in a school where for several years so many of them have had to
> simply survive in personal terms. Frequent changes of staff at
> lower levels had had a debilitating effect on these longer-serving
> teachers and a 'siege mentality' has developed.[4]

The head of a much larger school reported a year later:

> What parents should worry about is the insidious constant
> corrosion of petty violence and verbal violence . . . . . there is a
> real fear that a succession of trivial squabbles will eat into the
> necessary atmosphere of calm learning.[5]

This headmaster, as reported in *The Times*, went on to say that
the worst pupils were not necessarily those from the worst
backgrounds, just as the ablest pupils, as this book has stressed,
are not always those with the greatest home advantages. He
thought that a correlation between a tendency to violence in
school and a lack of communication between the pupil and his
father was clearly made out, and that trouble was generally
apparent in the junior school. He suggested that honest and
accurate records should be kept and shown to parents and that
every large school ought to be able to accommodate some of its
pupils if necessary in a satellite away from its main building
where positive therapeutic work could be done.

Law and order and the discipline necessary to obtain it is of
course an exceedingly important aspect of children's schooling
about which teachers can become very anxious. Among those
concerned with educational theory and development there has
been a conspiracy of silence on this subject. In ten years of
editing an educational journal I can remember only one un-
solicited contribution dealing with discipline and control. And
yet there is inevitably a number of children in a large non-

selective school whose behaviour causes disruption of one kind or another. In urban areas the authority of parents and the sanctions exercised over children by the community itself have weakened. Physical violence and crude verbal abuse are constantly featured in television programmes watched by children. Brutal, defiant, aggressive self-assertion is regularly presented to them as normal adult behaviour. All these circumstances create real difficulties in many places, especially for the very large all-ability school and especially where there is high staff turnover, an absence of well-defined school policy and of firm, competent but non-autocratic leadership.

School policy needs definition at all levels. It is not just a matter of formulating grandiloquent statements of intention—such as "the student should develop his autonomy by internalising those concepts which will enable him to create a new political reality." More important than any such rigmarole (quoted from a book review in a "progressive" journal) is the practical guidance over ordinary day to day issues which a coherent and well-understood policy can provide. Under what conditions, for instance, if at all, should pupils be allowed to chew gum in class, have their transistor radios on, play cards on the premises? What records should be kept? What steps should be taken to ensure punctuality, to maintain the level of noise below the point at which it obstructs the learning of the quietly studious or drives a sensitive teacher to distraction? Good schools will take trouble to make explicit their decisions and plans for action, and to explain them to pupils.

In many parts of the country children who constitute the top ten per cent of the ability range are now entering comprehensive schools at the age of 11 or 13, when they would previously have been entering (at 11) a school smaller in size and selectively recruited. This is a fact not simply of personal but of national importance. To suggest that the whole nature of a country's educational system should be governed by what is held to be best for the top ten per cent would be ridiculous. But it would be unacceptable to operate a system in which only the central mass of children were considered, and the case of those with special need, arising from extremes of ability or disability, was completely ignored. We have to find out therefore what kind of difficulties the abler children have to contend with in the non-selective neighbourhood secondary school of today; and then see what ought to be done for them.

The purest form of comprehensive dogma is that which insists on the single neighbourhood school to which all children in a particular area must go and in which all should stay for as long as possible. The size of such a school is not regarded as being of particular significance. It is held more important that no single parent or child should be favoured in any way, as would be the case if they were permitted choice of school, or if expenditure over and above that alloted by central and local government authorities was incurred in the education of a particular child.

The disadvantages of the neighbourhood school are well-known, particularly in North America. There are neighbourhoods where it is unlikely that many pupils will aspire towards the more challenging kind of secondary education and where it is unlikely that teachers will themselves live. The gains to be had from a teaching staff which identifies with the community in which their school is placed have been well illustrated in England by the success of schools situated in the new towns. The restriction of educational opportunity to what can be provided in the neighbourhood school is glaringly unfair to pupils of high ability who happen to belong to families living in the less desirable quarters of large towns. Only where amenities and housing conditions are reasonably equal can the neighbourhood school be regarded as an instrument of social justice.

The size of the school is another factor of importance and another example of the way the public has been misled. After the 1944 Act, parents were told that expert teachers and psychologists would decide which of the available secondary schools was the right one for their children. A little later parents living in the areas where comprehensive schools had been built were told that recondite but indisputable academic factors made it mandatory that their children should attend schools vastly greater in size than had been customary. What in both periods parents actually wanted were relatively small schools in which the pace and content of learning was adjusted as nearly as possible to the aptitudes and abilities of their particular children. They were not, and are still not, being given what they want.

Of all the elements in the education of the young the most vital is the teacher. This claim is no more disputed by the de-schooling faction than it is by the most die-hard traditionalist. The public wants teachers of good qualifications and experience and would pay for them more readily than it would for many other large items of public expenditure. The suggestion that those with the highest academic qualifications should teach the most academically gifted children seems as reasonable to most people as that the best musicians or the best bricklayers should teach those most eager and most apt for those skills. To disperse the best qualified teachers over the whole ability range and employ them in all levels of work indiscriminately is certainly bound to depress the standards attained at the highest level. This is one of the reasons why the more able pupil who attends a comprehensive school is at present likely to find his post-16 needs best served by a sixth form college or college of further education. Another reason is of course to be found in the general atmosphere of the place in which he wishes to learn. Various influences contribute to this hardly definable but always significant factor. However before examining the conditions that are likely to suit the more able from the age of 15 or 16 onwards a little more must be said about current anxieties over the formative earlier years.

A tendency in secondary education which followed the grammar school tradition was to push ahead in the early years with intensive factual learning which left little time for speculative enquiry or stimulus to the imagination. This was as much to be seen in language studies as in mathematics. It was wholly in the interests of the abler children that a strong reaction should have set in. There is of course a myth that grammar schools in the twentieth century are, or were, static institutions in which nothing changed. As with the public schools, the rate of change was very notable, although hostile critics naturally showed a tendency not to note it. Curriculum reform in the 1960s was largely the result of the activities and enterprise of those who had taught, or were still teaching, in grammar schools and independent secondary schools. These reforms were substantial in terms both of content and method. In fairness it should be recorded, however, that teachers in the new comprehensive schools were soon to show themselves just as capable of innovation and experiment, not merely in the management of large institutions, but also in curriculum development. Inevitably their creative ingenuity was largely devoted to the mainstream. No one, well informed about developments, can deny the real gains made in extending educational opportunity to the middle levels of ability. The sad thing is that such valuable advances should sometimes have been bought at the expense of the most able.

We have already referred to the impact of violence, of boorish standards of behaviour and of an irrational or barbarian outlook hostile to learning. There is real doubt as to whether enough teachers see these phenomena as the serious dangers that they are today. Occasionally, a modern comprehensive school seems to have resigned itself to the acceptance of very low standards in these matters. It is often the aim of teachers to adopt a friendlier and more sympathetic attitude to their less able pupils and to base their teaching on what seems relevant and not too unfamiliar to them. In so doing they tend to weaken some of the more positive influences which schools have been expected to exert. To many people education carries moral and social responsibilities and is concerned with lasting values and with standards of behaviour and taste. Such things are communicated less by the attitude that a teacher adopts to his pupils and more by what he really is as a person who has chosen a vocation in which self-expression, even self-revelation, is demanded. Perhaps more teachers today seem superficially on good terms with their pupils, but perhaps fewer have the time and certainty of purpose to become powerful influences in their pupils' lives. Such a teacher, vitiated by a total incapacity for self-criticism, was drawn by Muriel Spark in the character of

Miss Jean Brodie, who in 1931 taught the class of junior girls in the year before they passed into the senior section of an Edinburgh school. As a result of her teaching the "Brodie set" of six variously talented girls were

> vastly informed on a lot of subjects irrelevant to the authorised curriculum, as the headmistress said, and useless to the school as a school. These girls were discovered to have heard of the Buchmanites and Mussolini, the Italian Renaissance painters, the advantages to the skin of cleansing cream and witch-hazel over honest soap and water, and the word 'menarche'; the interior decoration of the London house of the author of *Winnie-the-Pooh* had been described to them, as had the love lives of Charlotte Brontë and of Miss Brodie herself. They were aware of the existence of Einstein and the arguments of those who considered the Bible to be untrue. They knew the rudiments of astrology but not the date of the Battle of Flodden, or the capital of Finland. All of the Brodie set, save one, counted on its fingers, as had Miss Brodie, with accurate results more or less.[6]

To stimulate and feed the curiosity of the mind and to stretch its powers of understanding are clearly prime duties of the teacher. Some believe that children around the age of 12 and 13 are more alert, curious and eager to learn than at any other age. Those with the native courage to explore the world in realms of thought and imagination, as well as in knowledge of its material properties, are at a critical stage in their development. This is the time when systematic teaching is important but no more so than the confidence and personal support which a sympathetic adult can give.

At this age good teaching involves intensive pupil initiation into the techniques of learning. To form the habit of working at home without teacher supervision; to read in order to acquire not only sensation but meaning; to stretch the mind so that it comes within reach of ideas hitherto beyond its range; to acquire skills in recording information, note-taking, the use of a library, the arrangement of facts and materials; to achieve standards of tidiness and order in the presentation of work, and the basic components of the power to communicate—all these are things the ablest children between the ages of 12 and 14 may learn from teachers, regardless of their subject specialisation. All also can be neglected by schools and many *are* neglected.

The background paper for the regional conferences organised by the Department of Education and Science in 1977 pointed out that the organisational arrangements of secondary schools never could ensure quality. "Many of the current disquiets," it went on, "over the achievements of schools in mathematics, sciences, modern languages and literacy arise directly from the lack in many schools of appropriately qualified and experienced teachers."[7] This indeed must be true, but even a teacher moderately equipped with specialised knowledge can open up a wide range of work and by personal example fire the enthusiasm of his pupils, provided that the general support of his colleagues is forthcoming and the atmosphere in which he works is conducive to serious learning. Too often in the early years of secondary education these conditions are not present. Teachers of mathematics, science and languages are on the whole convinced that their subjects require certain organisational arrangements, such as homogeneous teaching groups, which are unobtainable in many schools. Full time teachers of classical languages and of modern languages, other than French, are simply not wanted in a steadily growing number of secondary schools. In the Midlands about one school in five is able to offer Latin. It will soon be apparent to all that the sole hope of securing language teachers, "appropriately qualified" and secure "in their specialist knowledge", as the D.E.S. insists they should be, must come from former pupils of the independent schools. For there only, it seems, will serious language teaching from an early age be feasible. It may ultimately prove of advantage to the nation that over 100 of its best schools have recently been handed over to the independent sector.

Teaching and learning are adventurous occupations in which morale and motivation, as much as skill and expertise, are demanded. Many factors in modern comprehensive schools undermine the morale of those who teach the subjects where continuity is of paramount importance. In Latin or maths, for instance, the capacity to teach what lies ahead is governed by what has, or what should, already have been learned. The motivation of pupils is also dependent on the learning context, on the prevailing mood of the community. In mixed schools it is all too frequent that language is regarded as a subject for girls and science as a subject for boys, just as in the old-fashioned primary school boys' crafts and girls' crafts were separated out. Girls, more obviously than boys, seem to be affected, in terms of the effort they are prepared to exert, by general climates of opinion and by particular personal responses to individual teachers. Thus in schools where the discipline of learning and the values of a non-violent civilised society are absent, girls with academic or artistic ability will meet very restricted opportunities. In a school where graffiti, litter and damage to property are commonplace, where squalid physical conditions are permitted to exist because no one takes the trouble to alter them, it is improbable that aesthetic subjects will flourish or that social skills and attitudes to others, which, both on personal and political grounds young people need to learn, will be easily taught. It is not uncommon that in specialist rooms, where the standards of care and conservation are imposed by a teacher and valued by pupils, respect for civility, safety and pleasure in appearances is to be found. In the same school this sense of order and respect may be completely absent in the corridors, communal rooms and thoroughfares of the place. The adult atmosphere which, it is often claimed, 16 year olds appreciate in the college of further education, and do not find in an all-through comprehensive school, is produced by various factors, amongst them the presence, rather than the absence of authority, discipline and good order.

H.M. Inspectors have recently recorded an assessment of modern language teaching in 83 comprehensive schools. "In all too many language classes there was an atmosphere of boredom, disenchantment and restlessness, at times this developed into indiscipline of a kind which made teaching and learning virtually impossible."[8]

Even when conditions, both tangible and intangible, are good,

L

the ultimate examination success of the pupil aspiring to acceptable O-level results may be prejudiced by slow pace and a late start to the examination course. This is of course particularly marked where the break between schools comes as late as 14, leaving only five terms in which to prepare for the first public examination. Courses may have to be rushed and those taking them together may have had very different kinds of syllabus and teaching in their lower schools. Liaison between schools is seldom as good as it ought to be. The exercise of options in the case of the able pupil involves important and difficult considerations. Any kind of break in schooling between 11 and 13 adds to the problem. Good choices are generally made only when pupils have confidence in the advice of teachers, built on familiarity. In the same way a teacher is unlikely to give sound advice without a good knowledge of his pupil, derived from teaching him over a long period. It was rightly observed by the Dainton Committee, which reported in 1968 on the flow of young scientists and technologists into higher education, that great gains could come from ensuring that the majority of pupils in secondary education should come into *early* contact with good science teaching. Overwhelmingly the universities and polytechnics recruit scientists from those who opt for at least six periods of science teaching at about the age of 13. Unless they obtain a favourable impression of such studies before that age, they will choose something else when the moment of choice comes.

We now pass to the range of possibilities open to the able boy or girl at about the age of 16. Those with whom this book is concerned will have made up their minds on one point which will worry many of their contemporaries—whether to look for a job or to continue in full-time education. For reasons we have already discussed some promising students will have obtained lower O-level grades than their ability would have warranted, and some will have been diverted from entering at all in tough, linear subjects which have a high value in terms of future careers. Many boys will be without language qualifications, though well-equipped in science, and many girls, especially those attending mixed schools, will be under-achievers in mathematics, chemistry and physics. Indeed they may have dropped or never started these two sciences. Our children will have received some advice already on their career prospects. There is no established common policy about its nature, but it was estimated in 1973 that career implications of curricular choice are discussed with pupils and parents by 82% of secondary schools during the third year. It is, however, when a programme of A-level studies has to be thought out that pupils are in particular need of individual guidance from experienced teachers. "The teachers help us as much as they can," said one girl to an inspector engaged on the careers survey, "but the trouble is that there are too many of us and too few of them."

A vigorous controversy has been in progress for a number of years about general and specialised education for able pupils. Premature and excessive specialisation in a limited number of subjects all drawn from the same area of learning was already being condemned twenty years ago. Virtually nothing has been done on a national scale to alter it, although more students are now able to read for degrees which cross subjects boundaries, and to prepare for entry to higher education by taking A-levels in, for instance, an arts subject, a science subject, and one of the social sciences; or by combining mathematics, not with physics and chemistry as was conventional, but with history, geography or economics. It has been suggested that all pupils should continue to study mathematics to the end of their school days, just as all, in theory at least, are concerned with communication in speech and writing. But no prescription has been issued and no consensus has been reached. There is no school leaving certificate in England and Wales, only the record of the grade obtained in whatever subjects a pupil has chosen to attempt in the General Certificate or the Certificate of Secondary Education. These single subject examinations are normally taken by those who wish at the age of 16 and 18. A proposal that yet another possibility should be offered—a 17+ examination—is unlikely to be implemented in spite of our apparent national enthusiasm for external examining.

It still remains open to an able pupil to pursue his special lines of interest to the exclusion of subjects which make no appeal to him. He can go straight from school to higher education with no knowledge of a foreign language, no knowledge of history other than what he learned before the age of 13 and very little knowledge of mathematics or science. This sometimes appears shocking to enlightened people, particularly it seems to those who were trained as scientists. I think it need not be so. The most important matter for bright children is not the variety or the quality of their educational diet but its quality. We may define them as those capable of exercising their minds with abstractions and of using their imagination to reach out towards the adaptation or modification of things to make them suit specific purposes. Words would be one such thing, a constructional kit another, personal relations a third. Such children by these means can and should learn at school how to write, how to make and how to love—none of which are powers easily come by.

The question is whether the quality of their education will be enhanced by learning a little about much or quite a lot about a limited number of subjects, for instance the two or three chosen for study to A-level. Which alternative will be most helpful when it comes to using language, making things or forming loving personal relationships?

Without undertaking with enthusiasm the pursuit of knowledge in a self-chosen situation, I doubt whether any true experience of learning can be had. The quality of education seems to lie in the extent to which the person's imagination is challenged and his powers of independent thought extended. It is not the number of subjects studied, but the manner in which they are studied that affects these issues. If, because of a wide spread of studies, some area of learning can only be superficially observed by the student, he will see only what is pointed out to him. The chance of his acquiring the power to think through some aspect of the subject for himself is scarcely likely to occur. In later life it may be essential to pick up a smattering of knowledge of various kinds. The individual, under pressure to do so for practical ends, will not find it difficult or boring, but consider the enthusiastic adolescent on the threshold of the vast treasure house of learning. He will see things very differently.

From all that has been said about the nature of high ability there emerges a very powerful reason to sustain a right to specialise at school in a chosen subject. Not all the very able will necessarily choose to do so. Genuine all-rounders exist and will exert themselves in response to any call made on their energy. But more often what draws out the best student is the freedom to pursue his own bent, to obtain, while still young, a sight of his subject's distant frontiers.

A short-hand way of referring to the conflict in primary education is to speak of child-centred and teacher-centred approaches. In secondary education the dialectic seems to be between fact-oriented and frontier-oriented concepts of purpose —a reading of the present situation which I owe to R. A. Hodgkin. What happens is that one set of forces calls for an output of young people well-primed with basic information in fields of learning considered important to society at the present time. Overwhelmingly today the energies generated by our society are expended in an intricate structure of wealth production, distribution and consumption. The social contract which binds us together to this end entails also an elaborate organisation of public services. The ablest pupils of our schools are naturally expected to play their part in these great human affairs and their education is thought to be relevant and practical in so far as it contributes to their doing so.

There is, however, another view, conjoined in admission that schools have to be instruments of social purpose, but broader in its vision of what that concept implies. The supreme duty to society of the most able minds is to perceive, to criticise and to make better the conditions of human life. That these conditions have moral and spiritual, as well as political and economic dimensions, is plain to all who live outside ivory towers. The problem for schools is therefore that of introducing moral and spiritual experience into the lives of their pupils. There are many acclaimed methods of achieving this, but common to all is the necessity for stimulating emotional as well as intellectual or aesthetic response. The frontier concept of education points to the results of taking a student to somewhere near the limit of his capacity and, in another sense of the word, to a point as near the frontier of knowledge as his understanding can take him. On this frontier, to quote Hodgkin, "he is emotionally exposed and his competence of skill and of knowledge is fully stretched."

The image for those who know Hodgkin's two remarkable books[9] is of a young rock climber. It could equally be of the young mathematician trying to establish the validity of some creative impulse or simply playing chess against a good opponent. Fact-oriented secondary education is of course no more to be condemned than teacher intervention in primary schools. It should not, however, be permitted to dominate the aims and methods of the teacher. Able pupils must be given a glimpse of the educational frontier and taught the skills without which they will not possess the competence to maintain themselves there.

Before leaving school then we should expect the boys and girls with an evident capability for competent performance to have been offered the chance of as deep a study of a subject as can be provided. This means that schools in which such pupils are found must still be regarded as places where specialist teachers will operate as specialists.

A second thing of importance is that career opportunities should be kept wide open. Specialisation is not the same thing as type-casting. The ablest young people may well be just those most reluctant to commit themselves and most uncertain at 17 of what they want to be doing at 23. They will be served best, it has been claimed, if they can begin to approach at least one subject in the manner of a scholar and an enthusiast while still at school. Such a study should not of course constitute their whole educational programme, and its purpose should be rather to acquaint them with the process of learning than that they should acquire extensive factual knowledge for a competitive fact-oriented examination. If ever five subject passes in a public examination were to be demanded for entry into higher education, it is to be hoped that in the interests of the most able the preparation for such a programme would not be expected to occupy the whole of the student's time.

Finally there is the question of what should be done about moral and social values for the ablest group of young people towards the end of their school career. Traditionally the able have been expected to combine with their highly academic studies leadership, responsibilities in the social activities of the school and sometimes roles in discipline and government, particularly in boys' schools. These demands have tended to reduce the time and energy available for developing personal interests in, for instance, the arts and indeed in all directions other than those earning immediate social approval in a school community.

The heroes of Kipling's *Stalky & Co*—three boys in their last year at school—have no wish to play team games, to organise the lives of younger boys or to uphold the rule of law in the restricted context of the school. Instead one reads Ruskin, one writes poetry and the third leads the trio in elaborate tactical operations designed to deflate the dignity of masters and conventionally minded senior boys. Kipling's aim is to show the significance of self-determined values in the process of education. It is a point that should never be neglected, but it was a weakness of the English tradition that in public schools it often should have been.

On the other hand there is strength in the fact that the origin and much of the continuing tradition of English education is religious. Young people of intellectual ability may well attribute more to the powers of reason that they can actually deliver. Scientific materialism and philosophic realism may exert on them too strong an influence to be healthy. Life has dimensions which they are not likely as yet to have encountered.

The totalitarian state and the consumer-oriented society are both enemies to those apparently indestructible impulses in human nature which can set young people in search of some better vision of the world. Only when perspectives are enlarged by reference points to be found in religious history, art and

thought is that vision within human reach. An education without
ideals and aspirations larger than those of personal ambition is a
meagre offering.

CHAPTER XI

What Should be Done

This book began with the personal problems faced by exceptionally gifted children and their parents. This was followed by an attempt to point out the national importance of cultivating talent by differentiating educational targets and methods so that the ablest children are helped to realise their full potential. There is no reason to think that anything but a tiny minority of teachers would be unwilling to do this, if they knew how and were placed in situations where such differentiation was possible.

It has been argued here that two particular groups of children will suffer most if their special needs are ignored—they are first of all able children whose homes afford no support to educational ambition, and second the girls of all social classes with a potential for high performance in mathematics and science.

equality
of
opp.

Some members of our society are at a social and economic disadvantage. Justice for those so placed would seem to demand that their children should be educated in accordance with their abilities just as readily as the rest. It is also true that injustices are done to women and obvious that the more anarchic, the more politically inept our society becomes, the greater these will be. It would therefore on both counts be in the interests of efficiency and social justice to make better provision for the two groups of children indicated above. How should this be done?

The beginning must be lodged in the pre-school years. The quality of a society depends far more than our ancestors supposed on the nature of the relationships between parents and children in the first three years of a child's life. Play-groups, nursery classes and nursery schools provide important services for children but perhaps the opening they sometimes provide for the in-service training of young parents could become a more significant part of what they do. Certainly the claim of young parents on the resources devoted to welfare, advisory support, community care and adult education ought to carry top priority. We know enough now to know that some of the ills suffered by geriatrics can be traced back to infancy and might never have occurred but for ignorance years before.

Education is now seen as a life-long affair. Solid progress can only result from improvements carried out all along the front. Stages of education are inter-locking. We have so to distribute our efforts that there is educational validity in all that is done for the welfare of society. By this means it is possible to achieve a learning society in which personal fulfilment for all within a civilised social framework becomes the general aim.

Schools for young children in England and Wales have been much admired by recent visitors, particularly for an atmosphere and type of child/adult relationship which is often developed. Today some critics believe that these admired achievements have been won at the cost of denying attention to cognitive learning and the basic skills. There has thus been a demand for closer supervision over what is actually taught and for national tests of attainment. In infant and junior schools anxieties have arisen mainly because of poor results from the less able children. The interests of the more able are best served by broad, exploratory programmes of learning, rather than the narrow disciplines of the past.

Equally helpful to them is the growing development of teacher ability to promote individualised learning, which can of course be accelerated, rather than the class or group learning pattern, which may put a brake on their progress. The greatest emphasis is laid on this point in Dr. Ogilvie's study[1] of gifted children in primary schools. General library provision and the use of individual teaching aids are essential requirements. Powers of organisation, of stimulating children's interests and of maintaining detailed progress records are required from the teacher.

There are of course primary schools which well-informed parents of bright children would not want them to attend. But the reasons for this are more likely to be a particular school's specific weaknesses in staffing or management than because the educational foundations are shaky. Parents of highly talented children and those whose abilities suggest that they will eventually make good in higher education do however have two legitimate general causes of concern. They are well illustrated in a single case study from Dr. Ogilvie's survey.

P. was a boy who happened to attend a kindergarten where an educational psychologist, herself a parent, observed him and guessed his I.Q. to be around 165. He went later to his local primary school where there was much to interest him and a plentiful supply of books, games and musical activities. His family then moved to another district. Here he attended a school where he was regarded as a good quiet boy but where there was nothing that aroused his interest in the routine of classroom work and no "extras at all." At home as well as at school he became quiet, apathetic, even morose. After a useless interview with the headmaster, who regarded his parents' anxiety as a fuss about nothing, he was seen by an educational psychologist and his I.Q. turned out to be above 170 (Stanford Binet). His school, even with this information, found it impracticable to advance him by a year and in the end his parents resorted to private education.

Cases of this kind—and many of them involve the children of teachers—led to the formation of the National Association for Gifted Children. But it is not only those caring for the very high I.Q.'s who worry about the indifference of some primary schools to evidence of special aptitude for learning. Parents of children whose ability might not be outstanding, as measured by the accepted tests, but is certainly sufficient to place them in the top 6 to 8 per cent, will also contemplate the advantages of a private school. Their worries too will centre on the pace and the range of what is offered by the local primary school.

The case of P. also illustrates the alternative strategies which ought to be considered. They are applicable as much to I.Q.s around 130 as to those around 170. The first is generally described as enrichment. It entails the organisation of opportunities for outstandingly interested children to engage in academic and creative activities outside school hours. This is the kind of work which members of the N.A.G.C. are doing most to stimulate and indeed to organise. In various parts of the country and in any number of different ways, with many different agencies involved, enrichment programmes for gifted children are mounted after school, at week-ends and in the holidays. It is a growing movement, in which a number of local education authorities, teacher training organisations and voluntary enthusiasts are involved, but it has not yet spread sufficiently widely to do more than meet a fraction of the need. If enrichment is to become a telling factor in the education of children, more money would have to be laid out. Some of this will come from parents themselves and might be sought, too, from industry and other private sources. Money from public funds might be provided from a reduction in the large amounts spent on external examinations. It has been calculated that more is now spent on the administration, on related research and on fees than on the books needed to prepare for them. Yet nearly half the school population never present themselves for these elaborate national tests. To organise more opportunities outside the examinable areas of the curriculum and to endow prizes for original work in art, craft and creative writing, as in the City of Leicester, would seem to be far more profitable activities. The circulation with N.A.G.C. support of an "Explorers Unlimited" newsletter through which gifted children are kept informed about ways of furthering their interests and are put into communication with each other is a striking piece of enterprise. Correspondence courses and arrangements for volunteer private tutoring might be added to what is already provided. One can even imagine a national, "open school" on the lines of the Open University.

The second alternative was in P.'s case suggested by the educational psychologist. It is to expedite the progress of an able child either by providing an express route for him through the system, or by placing him together with a group nearer to his own mental age than to his chronological age. In the era of the 11+ some authorities permitted under-age candidates of marked ability to take the tests and proceed early to the grammar or technical school. In the original Leicestershire Plan for secondary organisation the same provision for the outstandingly gifted was made. In independent, direct grant and some grammar schools "high-fliers" were often recognised early. They were then "expressed" through the school, sometimes by a route which by-passed O-levels, and were entered a year early for A-levels and eventually for university scholarships. With due care exercised and a liberal interpretation of a balanced education, these practices were perfectly reasonable and often, if not always, in the true interests of the able child. Outside the independent sector, it is unlikely that such children could today take advantage of them.

The last resort then for the unsatisfied parents of a young child is the rare special school for children of exceptional talent or the independent school. The provision of the first by local education authorities is now absurdly forbidden except for music and ballet. The situation of the second remains where it was but is bound to be affected by inflation. Among the parents of able children are those who believe that an independent school would provide the best education for them. There could be many reasons for this belief and certainly the variety of independent schools, though many are for older children only, is remarkable. They offer a choice of single-sex or co-educational, boarding or day, provision. They may be old or comparatively modern establishments. They may be as large as the average comprehensive school or very small. Their origins are likely to lie in the particular concern for education of people with strong religious attachments—to the Roman Catholic, Anglican or

Methodist churches, to other forms of dissent including, rather notably, that of the Society of Friends or to the Jewish faith, or just to strong, but undenominational, ethical or academic conviction. Their characteristics are as varied as their origins.

Many parents believe that if they, or someone who wishes them well, could meet the cost it is to one of these schools that their gifted child should go. Among their reasons might be the thought that certain branches of learning will be better and more continuously tackled by them than by the state system with its regional variations and its breaks in continuity. These can occur at a number of possible points and cannot be foreseen by those who have to move their homes. The subjects affected are those which we have called linear—mathematics and languages in particular. It is sometimes believed that an early start to Latin, to at least one modern language and to the styles of learning most favoured in the "public" schools, must be made, particularly in the case of boys. In some instances, both for boys and girls, an independent school offers an all-through run from as early an age as 8 up to 18 or 19 but 11 or 13 is a more normal age of entry.

Whether or not a child should be placed in an independent school is a matter for private judgement and it would be foolish to base it on anything but the individual needs and nature of a particular child. Perhaps, however, some considerations are worth keeping in mind where a child with conspicuous general ability is concerned. The first of these is the tendency of too many teachers in the state sector to suppress the whole question of special treatment for special ability. For many this is unfamiliar ground and they are just not interested. The point was forcibly put by the headmaster of a comprehensive school, formerly a teacher at a direct grant school, when writing of ways in which schools like his should tackle the question of providing as appropriate an education for the very able as they did for those with special difficulties. "The first priority," he wrote, "must be to bring the question of giftedness out into the open, so that teachers will overcome the fear of being branded as 'élitist' if they as much as mention the most able."[3] Nearly every maintained secondary school, he points out, has a teacher in charge of remedial education, but few, if any, have a similar post for the opposite end of the ability range. To how many teachers in training is it suggested that they should make a special study of teaching very able children or see their life-work in that field? Men and women of intellectual distinction, attracted to the vocation of teaching, are today more likely to see their career prospects in the independent sector, in the residual grammar schools or colleges with a 16+ entry than in the all-through or lower tier comprehensive school.

A second factor of some moment is the more adjustable business-like, customer-oriented ethos of schools for which parents pay and from which children can be withdrawn. This is not just a matter of contrast between independent and maintained school, between fee-paying and free education. What I have in mind is readily available in colleges of further education, no doubt too in sixth form colleges, and it could often be found in the maintained grammar schools. It is a matter of giving attention to the individual needs of individual students, of making demands on their energies, keeping them up to the mark through the vigilance of a "course" tutor or form master or "house" tutor, and exercising a system of sanctions, if necessary. Good organisation in matters of this kind give a student confidence and a sense of security. He knows what he is expected to achieve and that those who teach are employed on his side for a particular purpose, not their own purpose, but one on which his future is dependent. Tests and records of his progress are what he is entitled to demand. He will expect a service conscientiously discharged to suit his personal requirements.

Some expressions of view by teachers and by their leaders and advisers have seemed to members of the public unacceptably arrogant. Paradoxically the independent sector, including the famous public schools, can give an impression of modesty and flexibility when some contemporary comprehensive schools do not. The Bullock Report recommended the introduction of a screening process by means of which the language attainment of all children entering the junior school should be systematically tested and recorded. It also suggested that standards of literacy should be monitored on a sample basis at the age of 11 and 15. These are the kinds of investigation from which much of value to individual children might be gained. They are steps which the public would welcome and is entitled to demand. As yet it is by no means clear that the politically organised part of the teaching profession would accept them.

Secondary education has been subjected to unprecedented strain by the laudable efforts of the past twelve years to achieve a massive re-organisation. The ground gained is far more extensive than that lost. Some large new schools have mastered difficult conditions, but on the whole the smaller, more modest establishment and the 11–16 rather than the 11–18 school has had most success. The best of all through comprehensives have more to offer than the average grammar school of the past, and the 11–16 comprehensive is generally a different class of school altogether in comparison with all but the most exceptional secondary school.

But the greatest problem raised by making the one type of school universal and obligatory is that a kind of mediocrity tends to be established and the standards set, and expectations entertained, are those adjudged suitable for average or below average pupils. This is to some extent because the ablest are absent, as there are not enough of them to go round while parents continue to find ways out of the state system. It is much more because the schools themselves, as at present organised and staffed, cannot bring the best out of their abler pupils. They have not made educational excellence, in the sense of high all-round achievement, with the highest priority attached to demanding academic and creative subjects, their main target. Gifted people in the arts, as well as in science and the humanities, are not to be attracted into teaching unless they have a reasonable prospect of meeting children whose special gifts for these things are recognised. Still less will they find themselves at home in institutions where the staff opinion, underlying the organisation of the work, is inimical to the needs and interests of those with the keenest minds and strongest enthusiasms. It has been suggested on the authority of the D.E.S. that in science, mathematics and technology there is no way of securing such teachers unless they are attracted into the profession from industry or commerce.[4]

Teachers in secondary schools are often too much stretched, too much under stress, inadequately prepared for their work or wrongly motivated by the leadership they receive. They are influenced by outmoded notions of the society in which they live—and so unfortunately are their pupils. The point is well made by an educational psychologist writing on a common attitude among able girls. "When selecting careers they set themselves lower standards than their ability warrants. Like all normal people they wish to be accepted by society and are therefore forced to compromise, accepting lower standards for themselves."[5]

Planning for the future must now be a process of repairing damage done by recent changes and of working out radical reforms. The steps that should be taken will be to the benefit of all children, not merely those with the most conspicuous ability, but the present weaknesses needing to be remedied have their most serious effect in the higher ranges of ability. Among the many drawbacks to large, complicated secondary schools is the strange fact that the ablest, most experienced teachers are often too occupied by administrative duties to do any teaching at all. The efforts of all secondary schools—in areas where this is allowed—to grow sixth forms and offer the number of subjects required to keep up with some rival establishment, have led to an absurdly wasteful distribution of the most highly qualified teachers. One might expect institutions that care for children to be bound together in material support like the hospitals, but this is not in fact the case. Efforts have been made in some areas to assemble the resources of schools and colleges of further education into single educational units, placing at the disposal of all within the area a great range of courses, academic and vocational. In Birmingham, where small secondary schools have been retained, advanced teaching is provided not by each individual school but by the consortium into which the schools

are formed.[6] Elsewhere the sixth form college may prove a
successful means of securing suitable levels of work for the
abler 16 year olds. The single secondary school has to become a
less exclusive, less self-preservative institution. It exists only to
perform a limited spread of services. There needs to be close
liaison with other agencies and free exchange for talented pupils
into centres of academic and artistic excellence. The future lies
with co-operative structures like the European Economic
Community and not with isolationist, go-it-alone independence.

It is therefore from the point of view of those with whom we
are concerned nothing less than a tragedy that the former
direct-grant schools are now independent and only to be regarded
as part of the national provision in so far as local education
authorities continue to pay the fees for children who are
qualified for the kind of education they provide. In education
the present government has nationalised nothing and de-
nationalised 119 schools. These schools, and indeed all independent schools possessing educational quality and worthwhile
resources, ought of course to be within a national system
contributing to the educational welfare of all. If the quality of
education is regarded as a true national objective, then we must
broaden our vision and reduce the influence of vested interests
and obsolete political prejudice.

Perhaps the single most important step would be firmly to
attach to academic learning the high value it has always had to
fight for in the history of English (though not of Scottish)
education. This is not simply a matter of restoring what once
was; in fact English schools have only spasmodically and in
some particular instances been regarded as primarily concerned
with intellectual development. Instead they have been seen as
instruments for the training of character, the correction of moral
evils, the production of various grades and types of individuals,
thought to be required by the emerging social and economic
structure. This is well illustrated by looking back at the different
kinds of schooling enjoyed by Keynes, Wells and Kipling. The
first was prepared at Eton and Kings for social and political and
artistic leadership; the second determinedly dedicated by his

mother to the role of shop assistant and educated in accordance with that ambition; the third attended, by chance rather than deliberate choice, an Imperial Service College set up with precisely the objective that its title indicates.

A shift from social and curatorial objectives towards the primacy of learning would demand changes of outlook less far-reaching, as we have seen, in the case of primary than in secondary education. The critical years in which the most serious mistakes are now made are not those spent in the junior school, but in the middle school or in the early years of the large comprehensive. We need a new outlook among teachers and a new set of specialists, trained to work with the 11 to 15 age range. Such people are today in extremely short supply. Able students of education see themselves either as future professional teachers of young children, or else as devoting themselves to the levels of work predicated by O and A-level examinations. It is vital that organisation and styles of teaching, capable of laying good academic foundations and habits of work, should be discovered and should be put into effect, during these middle years. The alternative can only be a continuing deterioration of standards at all levels, particularly in such subjects as languages and mathematics. Those affected will be the more able children on whom so much of the future depends.

All this implies a new look at old and controversial issues such as the streaming, setting and testing of pupils. It calls for bold innovation, such as the setting up (as in Israel) of special classes for the highly gifted in some of the ordinary schools.[7] The contents of the curriculum, the basic core of learning for all, optional subjects, time allocations, express routes for the most able, the school leaving examination—all these matters have to be reviewed and in many instances present practices would have to undergo radical change.

Discrimination between levels of ability and more exact definition of targets would themselves involve a necessary move towards closer checks on the expenditure of money, time and energy. This is an important direction for reform to take. Resources have been seriously wasted in part because schools have attempted to do more than can today be legitimately and economically expected of them. The public expects that education funds should be spent on teaching and learning and is entitled to a voice in defining exactly what this means. No individual school, from which children can be withdrawn only with difficulty, should be permitted to decide this for itself, regardless of outside opinion. Much could, however, be gained if local authorities or central government took the initiative in setting up experimental schools for research purposes, recruiting pupils on a volunteer basis.

Such developments would reflect a whole new climate in education, favourable to experiment, to freedom of choice, to independence of judgment, to co-operation between establishments, to the breaking down of barriers between parents and teachers, between schools and further education, between the public and the private sectors. In spite of die-hard resistance in some quarters and a small measure of unhelpful legislation, such developments are indeed taking place. Here and there the future can be seen and seen to work. The present Minister of Education, Mrs. Williams, has already indicated her hope that centres of excellence with high academic and intellectual standards should be found within the national secondary system. To a reasonable person it can hardly matter whether these are called comprehensive schools or not. The sole criterion should be that they are open to all the talents. It would be wise and economical to base some of what is to be provided for able children on former grammar and direct grant schools. Nor need it be beyond the capacity of unprejudiced good sense to bring the best inpendent schools into a working relationship with the public sector, as has been so effectively done already in Wiltshire, where Lavington School (ex-secondary modern) and Dauntsey's School (ex-direct grant) have worked out a happy partnership, not to aggrandise either school or to make any political point, but to serve the interests of young people which, they have remembered, is what education is all about.

Differences in the ability to learn are facts of life; differences in the will to learn are no less obvious. Our feelings about the basic principle of equality, however strong (and strong they ought to be) have to be reconciled with what commonsense and common fairness demand—that the able child be helped forward to the limit of his or her capacity. Equality cannot be procured by educational policies alone; and effective learning, which justice demands, can only be organised on the principle of differentiating between types and degrees of talent.

Notes

Chapter I

1 E. M. Hitchfield—*In Search of Promise* Longman 1973
2 G. B. Shaw—*Everybody's Political What's What* Constable 1944
3 David Hopkinson—'Controversy in Education' in *1870 – 1970* HMSO 1970
4 *Black Paper Two. The Crisis in Education* London 1969
5 Report of Committee on Higher Education (Robbins) HMSO 1968
6 Alvin Toffler *Future Shock* Bodley Head 1970
7 E. H. Erikson *Childhood and Society* Penguin 1965
8 *Half our Future* Report of the Central Advisory Council (Newsom) HMSO 1963

Chapter II

1 Matthew Arnold *A French Eton* London 1863
2 Arnold Toynbee *A Study of History* Vol. IV Oxford 1939
3 Michael Young *The Rise of the Meritocracy* Thames & Hudson 1961
4 Report of the Central Advisory Council (Spens) HMSO 1938
5 *15–18* Report of the C.A.C. (Crowther) HMSO 1959
6 P. B. Medawar *Two Conceptions of Science* Penguin

Chapter III

1 Eric Ogilvie *Gifted Children in Primary Schools* MacMillan 1973
2 James Conant *The American High School Today* McGraw-Hill 1959
3 Philip Magnus *Gladstone* John Murray 1954
4 E. M. Hitchfield *In Search of Promise* Longman 1973
5 D. W. MacKinnon *Personality Assessment* ed. B. Semeonoff Penguin 1966
6 Liam Hudson *Contrary Imaginations* Methuen 1966

Chapter IV

1 S. A. Bridges *Gifted Children and the Brentwood Experiment* Pitman 1969
2 N. R. Tempest *Teaching Clever Children* Routledge 1974
3 L. M. Terman *Genetic Studies of Genius*—Stanford Univ. Press
    Vol. 1 1925
    Vol. 4 1947
    Vol. 5 1959
4 *A Language for Life*—Report of the Committee of Enquiry (Bullock) HMSO 1975
5 J. P. Guilford 'Three Faces of Intellect' *American Psychologist* Vol. 14 1959
6 J. W. Getzels and P. W. Jackson—*Creativity and Intelligence* Wiley 1962
7 L. Hudson *Frames of Mind* Methuen 1968
8 M. A. Wallach and N. Kogan *Modes of thinking in Young Children* Holt, Rinehart and Winston 1965
9 T. Husen *Social Class and Educational Achievement* Educational Research Vol. 10 1968
10 M. Kellmer Pringle *Able Misfits* Longman 1970
11 E. M. Hitchfield *In Search of Promise* Longman 1973
12 J. B. Shields *The Gifted Child* N.F.E.R. 1968

Chapter V

1 G. W. Parkyn *Children of High Intelligence* O.U.P. 1948
2 Davie, Butler & Goldstein *From Birth to Seven* Longman 1972
3 L. Hudson *Contrary Imaginations* Methuen 1966
4 E. Hoyle & J. Wilks *Gifted Children and their Education* Department of Education & Science 1974
5 E. M. Hitchfield *In Search of Promise* Longman 1973
6 S. A. Bridges *I.Q.–150* Priory Press 1973

Chapter VI

1 R. F. Harrod *Life of J. M. Keynes* Macmillan 1951
2 H. G. Wells *Experiment in Autobiography* Vol. 1 Gollancz 1934
3 Charles Carrington *Rudyard Kipling. His Life and Works* Macmillan 1955
4 Rudyard Kipling *Something of Myself* Macmillan 1937

Chapter VII

1 Vera Brittain—*Testament of Youth* Gollancz 1933
2 Margaret Mead—*Blackberry Winter* Angus and Robertson 1972
3 *Standards of Reading* 1948–1956 HMSO 1957
4 K. B. Start and B. K. Wells *The Trend of Reading Standards* N.F.E.R. 1972
5 Report of the Consultative Committee on the Primary School HMSO 1931
6 *Primary Education* HMSO 1959
7 *Children and their Primary Schools*—HMSO 1967
  Vol. I Report
  Vol. II Research and Surveys
8 E. M. Hitchfield *In Search of Promise* Longman 1973
9 J. C. Barker Lunn—*Streaming in the Primary School* N.F.E.R. 1970
10 Burstall *et al. Primary French in the Balance* N.F.E.R. 1975
11 Frances Stevens *A Place for Learning* Hutchinson 1974
12 *15 to 18* Report of the Central Advisory Council HMSO 1959
13 Public Schools Commission—Second Report Vol. 1 HMSO 1970
14 *Curricular Differences for Boys and Girls*—Education Survey 21 HMSO 1975
15 Mary Warnock 'Towards a Definition of Quality in Education' in R. S. Peters (ed) *The Philosophy of Education* O.U.P. 1973

Chapter VIII

1 D. W. Winnicott—*The Child, the Family and the Outside World* Pelican 1964
2 Tom Hart—*Safe on a Seasaw*—Quartet 1977

Chapter IX

1 *Children and their Primary Schools,* HMSO 1967
2 E. Holmes *What Is and What Might Be* Constable 1911
3 John Blackie *Inside the Primary School* HMSO 1967
4 *Primary Education*—suggestions for the consideration of teachers HMSO 1959
5 *A Language for Life* HMSO 1975
6 *Mathematics in Primary Schools,* Schools Council Curriculum Bulletin No. 1 HMSO 1968
7 Edith Biggs, 'Progress in Primary Mathematics', *Trends in Education, 16* 1969

8 T. Husen *International Study of Achievement in Mathematics* Stockholm 1967
9 S. H. Froome, 'The Mystique of Modern Maths', *Black Paper Two* London 1969
10 J. S. Bruner *The Relevance of Education* Allen and Unwin 1972
11 A. B. Clegg (Ed.) *The Changing Primary School* Chatto and Windus 1972
12 R. L. James 'Mathematics in Primary Schools', *Trends in Education* 1975/4
13 *School Geography in the Changing Curriculum,* Education Survey No. 19 HMSO 1974
14 C. Burstall, *et al. Primary French in the Balance* N.F.E.R. 1975
15 D. H. Lawrence *Sons and Lovers* London and New York

Chapter X

1 *The Road to the Sixth Form* HMSO 1951
2 *Careers in Education in Secondary Schools* Education Survey No. 18 HMSO 1973
3 R. Mitson and M. Holder—'Comprehensive education within a Community Centre'—*Forum* Vol. 16 No. 3
4 Margaret Maden—'The young teacher in the secondary school' *Trends in Education* 1975/4
5 Michael Marland—*The Times* January 1977
6 Muriel Spark—*The Prime of Miss Jean Brodie* Macmillan 1961
7 *Educating our children*—Four subjects for debate, D.E.S. 1977
8 *Modern Languages in Comprehensive Schools*—HMSO 1977
9 R. A. Hodgkin *Reconnaissance on an Education Frontier* O.U.P. 1970 *Born Curious* John Wiley 1976

Chapter XI

1 E. Ogilvie *Gifted Children in Primary Schools* Macmillan 1973
2 Explorers Unlimited Newsletter, Ed. Anna Comino-James, Four Gables, Village Road, Denham, Bucks.
3 *Looking to their Future*—News Letter of the National Association for Gifted Children. 1 South Audley Street, London W.1
4 Times Educational Supplement—15th October, 1976
5 Phyllis M. Pickard *If you think your child is gifted*—Allen and Unwin 1976
6 B. Denton 'The development of consortia' in *Trends in Education* 1975/2

7 N. Butler, 'Israel's First Experiment in Special Classes for Gifted
   Children Within Regular Schools' in *Gifted Children—Looking to
   their Future,* Latimer with N.A.G.C., 1976